ASIAN AMERICANS
OF ACHIEVEMENT

ANNA SUI

ASIAN AMERICANS OF ACHIEVEMENT

Margaret Cho

Daniel Inouye

Maxine Hong Kingston

Michelle Kwan

Ang Lee

Bruce Lee

Maya Lin

Yo-Yo Ma

Isamu Noguchi

Apolo Anton Ohno

I.M. Pei

Anna Sui

Amy Tan

Vera Wang

Kristi Yamaguchi

Jerry Yang

ASIAN AMERICANS
OF ACHIEVEMENT

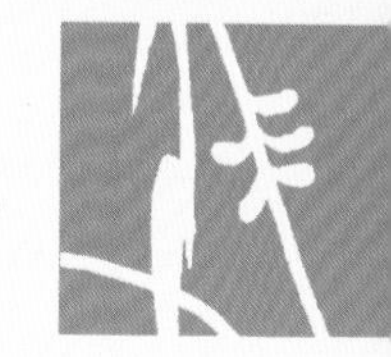

ANNA SUI

SUSAN MUADDI DARRAJ

Anna Sui

Chelsea House
An imprint of Infobase Publishing
132 West 31st Street
New York, NY 10001

Library of Congress Cataloging-in-Publication Data
Darraj, Susan Muaddi.
Anna Sui / Susan Muaddi Darraj
p. cm. — (Asian Americans of achievement)
Includes bibliographical references and index.
ISBN 978-1-60413-570-1 (hardcover)
1. Sui, Anna—Juvenile literature. 2. Women fashion designers—New York (State)—New York—Biography—Juvenile literature. I. Title. II. Series.
TT505.S943D37 2009
746.9'2092—dc22
[B] 2009014608

Chelsea House books are available at special discounts when purchased in bulk quantities for businesses, associations, institutions, or sales promotions. Please call our Special Sales Department in New York at (212) 967-8800 or (800) 322-8755.

You can find Chelsea House on the World Wide Web at http://www.chelseahouse.com

Series design by Erika K. Arroyo
Cover design by Alicia Post

Printed in the United States of America

Bang EJB 10 9 8 7 6 5 4 3 2 1

This book is printed on acid-free paper.

CONTENTS

1

The Point of No Return

Living in New York City in 1981 was tough for Anna Sui. She was in her mid-20s and working long hours for various fashion designers. In one sense, it was a fulfillment of her childhood dream: to work in fashion in the world's busiest and most stylish city. However, she had always hoped to design her own clothing—to express her own tastes and style—rather than work for someone else.

Upon arriving in New York City in 1973, Sui studied at the elite Parsons School of Design until 1975. Although she was excited to be living in New York and a long list of notable fashion designers were Parsons alumni, Sui did not find her course work very inspirational. She thought she would have a better chance to learn the fashion business if she began to work.

When she left Parsons, a classmate told her about a job opening in the field. Sui applied and was hired by Erica Elias to design clothing for Charlie's Girls, a junior sportswear company. Elias saw something youthful and hip in Sui's fashion sense. At Charlie's Girls, Sui had ample room for growth.

"I was in heaven," Sui recalled in an essay she wrote for *Newsweek*. "That was probably the best job I could have ever landed because Erica gave me my very own design room to work in." Her job allowed her access to several resources, including her own sewing crew and a draper, and an opportunity to work on various types of clothing. "It [the company] had five different divisions where I could do swimwear, sportswear, and sweaters," Sui said. "I learned how to do everything."

She recalled Elias being "the toughest boss" she ever had, which she meant as a compliment. Elias "demanded perfection and thorough research," and Sui applied herself to the rigorous work, arriving earlier and leaving later than anyone else. Her work ethic was based on her aspirations—she truly wanted to be successful in the fashion industry, and she was willing to put in as many hours as needed to achieve her goal.

Sometimes, however, the end result does not match the hard work. Charlie's Girls collapsed after only a year and a half. Despite the bad luck, Sui still came out of the situation more experienced than she had been. According to the article "Sui Generis," "Sui learned invaluable lessons about the fabric market, how and where to get the best quality at the best price. This knowledge, she feels, is essential to a successful design house." The inexperienced student was now an industry employee with 18 months of experience at a design company. Sui was slowly beginning to build up her résumé.

She immediately found work at similar companies, such as Glenora. During those years, while she worked busily for these companies, most of which designed junior sportswear, Sui carved out time in her schedule to design her own clothing. Whenever she had some down time, she would sketch out patterns for dresses, suits, and separates. The sketches were usually inspired by whatever interest she had at the time, whether it derived from music, art, or something she had seen in a night-club or at a party.

She always had a unique perspective on fashion, primarily based on the influences of the 1960s and 1970s. Sui loved the hippie styles of the 1960s, which were marked by loose, flowing, comfortable designs and natural textures, as well as the rock-'n'-roll fashions of the 1970s, featuring rich fabrics like velvets and leather and bold, assertive looks. From the two eras, Sui developed a funky, unified look that best expressed her own personality.

Of course, the early 1980s had its own influence on Sui's tastes. This was the beginning of the pop-rock movement, with musical stars like Madonna just emerging. In New York City, this look first became apparent on the club scene, the network of dance clubs like Studio 54, the Palladium, and Danceteria, where some of the most innovative fashions could be seen on display. Sui and her friends frequented the clubs often, and the style and clothing of the other clubbers often inspired the young designer.

In 1981, Sui began to toy with the idea of launching her own clothing line. Her mind was filled with ideas that longed to be brought from paper to reality, and she had access to machines, fabrics, and other resources. Though she worked in the fashion business, she actually had little idea how to begin, so she stayed close to home—in other words, she started in the living room of her apartment. In one corner of the loft-like space, she set up a workstation and began to make and sew clothing, bringing her designs to life.

The next step was to market some of her designs. Again, she had no idea how to accomplish this. She asked some of her friends, who were also artists, about marketing. Some of them happened to be jewelry designers and sold their crafts at fashion trade shows. They encouraged Sui to share their booth space at an upcoming show, the Boutique Show, and she accepted the offer. She prepared five clothing items to display at the event, which is one of the most important shows in New York City.

A BREAKTHROUGH

Fashion trade shows are the way in which people hoping to make their name in the industry showcase their designs, with the aim of generating interest in their clothing. Buyers from retail stores attend the shows to keep themselves updated on the latest fashions and the most exciting new designers. During the 1981 Boutique Show, Sui was thrilled to receive orders for her clothes from the fashion retail giants Macy's and Bloomingdale's. The sales were a major coup for an emerging designer, and Sui could not help but think that her business aspirations had been confirmed.

Even better news awaited. Macy's later featured one of Sui's dresses in a major advertisement it placed in *The New York Times*. The advertisement gave Sui a sudden and tremendous amount of exposure. She was excited and began to work on her clothing line during every minute of her spare time to fill the orders that were coming in.

The ad in *The New York Times* and the sales to Macy's, however, gave Sui and her designs a little too much exposure. In fact, it caused a significant problem at her full-time job. At the time, she was working for a company called Simultanee, a women's sportswear design firm. The company's owner saw the ad and recognized Sui's work. He confronted her and told her that she was only allowed to design for his company, not for anyone else—including herself. It is standard practice when a fashion company employs a designer that the designs produced are owned by the company, not the individual. Sui, however, felt that she had a right to design clothes for herself. Nonetheless, her employer insisted that she make a difficult choice—she could design only for Simultanee or be fired from the company.

Anna Sui acknowledged the applause from the audience after her runway show in February 2009 during Fashion Week in Manhattan. She had come a long way from the days when she was creating clothes in the living room of her apartment.

As Sui bluntly phrased it years later, "So I got fired." She added in another interview, "The decision was made for me at that point."

Though she recalls it today in a cavalier way, the decision was a terrifying prospect for the budding fashion designer. Living in New York City was very expensive, and she was sacrificing her sole steady source of income to do—what? Sew dresses in the corner of her living room? Though the orders she received were encouraging, the profits she earned were not enough to support her financially.

But there was no going back now. Sui spent her last paycheck from Simultanee to buy enough fabric to fill her next set of orders. She delivered the clothes, got paid, and then used those earnings to buy the fabric for her next set of orders. This paycheck-to-paycheck cycle was scary, and she worried about what would happen to her fledgling business if the orders were to dry up. To prevent that, she continually designed and made new items. She also displayed her clothing at more trade shows, where she gave herself the necessary exposure to more retail buyers. She also began to market herself by making sales calls to buyers and retail outlets, though she did not garner much success in this way until she was able to afford to hire a sales representative. With a professional handling her sales, Sui could focus on what she was good at: creating her one-of-a-kind, funky designs.

Despite her promising beginning, she would need a lot of inspiration—and luck—to succeed in one of New York's toughest businesses.

2

A Novelty Girlhood

Detroit, Michigan, is hardly known for its fashion culture. In fact, for decades, the city—known as the "Motor City"—has been the headquarters of the U.S. automobile industry, with the existence of companies like Ford, General Motors, and Chrysler. Indeed, reflecting on where she grew up, Anna Sui has said, "You have to focus on your dreams even if they go beyond common sense. . . . How could this young girl from the suburbs of Detroit become a success in New York? It was always that dream."

Her parents were both born in China. They lived and studied in Paris, France, where they met. Paul Sui was a student of structural engineering, and Grace, who became his wife, studied painting. They married in Paris, where their first child, a boy, was born.

Anna's parents enjoyed traveling and loved seeing the world. In fact, they were quite global in their view of things. This partly stemmed from the fact that Grace's father was a diplomat and traveled often, so Grace herself was exposed to

Western as well as Eastern cultures. The Suis wanted to ensure that their own children had a global view of the world and were exposed to other cultures, not just to Chinese culture and traditions.

"After they married," Anna once wrote, "they traveled throughout Europe for three years and finally settled in the United States." In Dearborn, outside of Detroit, Paul began an engineering career and Grace took care of their home and their growing family. Anna was born on August 4, 1955, and her younger brother was born not long after.

The Suis' home was decorated with artifacts and items from all over the world. Sui credits her parents' backgrounds and love of travel with influencing her and shaping her personality. "I get the business side from my father and the artistic side from my mother," she wrote in the *Newsweek* essay. "Hearing them talk about all the different places they had lived prepared me for thinking globally. This perspective took away any fears of being able to function in a foreign country. Their experiences were a gift to me."

The result was that Anna grew up in a household in which art was appreciated and a sense of adventure was valued. Their suburb, Dearborn, had communities of ethnic minorities, such as Arab Americans, African Americans, and other groups. But there were not many Chinese families or a large Asian population in general. "We were the only Chinese family in my neighborhood when I was growing up, and I was never a part of the Chinese community," Sui recalled in an interview with the *Toronto Star*.

THE SOLE GIRL

The Suis had three children—two boys and Anna. She insists that she never received any special attention as the family's only daughter, but instead she played with her brothers and their friends, doing typical boy things. "Anna idolized her

Anna Sui spent some time with her family before her show during Fashion Week in September 2007. With Anna were *(from left)* her father, Paul; her mother, Grace; and her brothers, Eddy and Bobby. Anna's parents were born in China and met while studying in Paris. They made sure their children were exposed to cultures from around the world.

brothers," the article "Sui Generis" said, "tagging along and agreeably playing boys' games. The only feminine aspects of Sui's girlhood seem to have been playing with Barbie dolls and being obsessed with the color lavender."

Still, Anna had gotten the idea in her head that she wanted to be a fashion designer. "When I was 4 years old, I was already talking about becoming a designer. I'm not exactly sure where I got that notion. It was probably something I saw on television. It seemed like a very glamorous life," she wrote in *Newsweek*.

Her parents had a very practical and direct way of pointing out her talents. In one story Sui tells, she was making cookies as a child and having a difficult time. (Till now, she claims that she does not and cannot cook.) Her mother, who was watching her, said bluntly, "Cooking isn't for you. Develop other talents."

Being a girl among two brothers did not hinder her early interest in fashion. In fact, she even manipulated the typical boyish games to suit her own, more stylish instincts. When she and her brothers played with toy soldiers, she would persuade them to dress up the soldiers and her own dolls and recreate the "red carpet" fashion show of the Academy Awards. "I would play with the neighborhood boy and we took tissue paper and made gowns out of the tissue paper," she said of other childhood memories. She enjoyed fashioning dresses and outfits from the tissue paper, then finding other materials to accessorize the looks.

Her mother and father enjoyed and encouraged Anna's creativity. When she became older, Anna learned to sew and began to make many of her own clothes. In seventh grade, she earned a reputation for being chic and stylish among her classmates because she never wore the same outfit twice for the entire school year. "I wanted to be best dressed in my class," she said of that year in an interview with the *National Post.* She went on to describe how she achieved that goal:

> I knew how to sew and I'd go shopping with my mom every weekend. I would find remnants and fabrics and I would make new little skirts or shift dresses. My favorite outfit was from a Vogue designer pattern I bought that was so hard to make. It had all these interfacing and handmade buttonholes, which I didn't really know how to do. I just looked at the directions and did my best. It was in linen, and it was a pale blue paisley. And I remember I used the remnant of the fabric and pasted it on top of a pair of shoes with glue so I had a whole matching outfit. I figured out how you could stretch the fabric and glue it down. I just thought

> that was the coolest thing in seventh grade—having matching shoes. I don't think my teachers knew what to think of me.

Besides loving fashion, Anna also showed an early liking for fantasy literature and art. One of her favorite books as a young child was *The Lion, The Witch, and the Wardrobe*, written by C.S. Lewis as part of his *Chronicles of Narnia* series. "[The novel] was my favorite," Sui recalled in *New York* magazine. "My English teacher in sixth grade gave me an A-minus on my book report, and she said, 'You have to start reading more adult books.' It broke my heart."

Anna's parents soon grew worried that their daughter's ambitions to be a fashion designer were quite serious, and they encouraged her to consider other fields and careers. Part of their concern was how fickle the fashion industry was; designers tried to get started and failed all the time. Even successful designers could have a bad season and watch their business suffer. Paul and Grace Sui urged their only daughter to consider other careers that would be more stable and allow her to have a financially balanced future.

After all, they knew that she had a lot of potential. From a young age, Anna was focused, intelligent, and hard-working—traits her parents had passed along to her. She did well in school, especially taking an interest in her history classes. Her older brother was also bright and had a reputation as "the smartest kid in school," she said. According to "Sui Generis," her mother once asked Anna, "Why do you want to design dresses when you have brains?"

PASSION AND EARLY INFLUENCES

Despite her parents' misgivings, Anna continued to pursue her passion for style, even with a studious and intellectual rigor. She started what she calls her "genius files," clipping pictures from magazines and catalogs that inspired her with ideas for new designs. Thus she created her own fashion archives, which she would refer to for the rest of her career.

Being Asian American

A GLOBAL VISION

Unlike other Asian-American fashion designers, Anna Sui does not see herself as having been significantly impacted by her Asian heritage. Part of the reason may be that her parents are very international people, having spent much time in Europe and the United States. Also, Sui grew up in Dearborn, Michigan, where there was not a sizeable Asian community. In fact, being the only Chinese person in her neighborhood made her feel special. "Everyone knew who I was. Everyone knew who my family was, and it set us apart," she said in an interview with CNN.

As an adolescent, Sui learned to fit in with the other kids her age at school, and to enjoy what they did: rock-'n'-roll music, fashion trends, dancing, and more. It is those same influences that have helped to make her a successful designer and the Anna Sui brand a global one. Everything she designs and creates—from clothing to perfume to makeup and even to cell phones—is infused with her personal interests and favorite pursuits, such as rock music and roses.

Perhaps that success is also due to the fact that she does not lock herself into a particular ethnic identity: Instead, Americans of all ethnic backgrounds can find their own forms of self-expression by wearing her designs.

Sui does admit, however, that she has what she refers to as "a Chinese vision": "People say that the color palette that I work with is very Chinese. I think even the prints that I'm attracted to.

It was during her childhood and teenage years, growing up in Detroit's suburbs, that Anna developed a clear sense for and appreciation of the things that would influence her later as a

Certainly the peony, which is on the packaging of the skin-care: I think I'm very Oriental," she told CNN. Sui attributes this innate attraction she feels toward "oriental" designs, fabrics, and objects to the fact that her parents admired such things as well, so she learned to associate them with beauty.

Despite not feeling so tied to the Asian community, Sui has done a stellar job in terms of cross-appeal. For example, Sui appeals to the Asian market as much as she does to the American and European markets—perhaps more so. The Isetan company, a major department store in Japan, markets many of her product lines, and her boutiques in Japan, South Korea, China, Singapore, Thailand, Taiwan, and the Philippines are popular and profitable. In China and other parts of Asia, the Anna Sui brand is always in demand, and she has worked with Asian companies like Samsung and Sanrio to help design other products, including toys and cell phones.

Although Sui did not grow up entrenched in the Asian or specifically the Chinese-American community, she does try to maintain her ties with her parents' homeland. For example, she visits the Sui family gravesite in China every year. Still, she naturally feels like more of an outsider than a native, since she was born in the United States. "They see me as American," she said in the *International Herald Tribune*. "If you are not born there and don't live there, they call you 'bamboo.' Chinese on the outside, but nothing inside."

designer. Though she hailed from a Chinese-American family, she did not feel—as she said—tied to the Chinese community. Because hers was the only Asian family in their neighborhood, Anna's Chinese background and ethnicity "made her more of a novelty than the object of racial hostility." While she was always "different" from her friends in school and the other kids in the neighborhood, she never felt ostracized, discriminated against, or unwelcome. In fact, she always felt that she "fit in" to American culture.

It was the most American thing of all that inspired her more than anything else in these early years: rock-'n'-roll music.

Growing up during the 1960s and 1970s, Anna could not have escaped the influence of rock 'n' roll. Nor did she want to—in fact, she embraced it.

Rock 'n' roll developed in the 1960s as an outgrowth of other popular types of music, like rhythm and blues, jazz, and even country music. It has its origins in songs like those of Elvis Presley, Chuck Berry, and other artists of the 1950s. The main instrument in rock music is the electric guitar, which gives the music its catchy, edgy rhythms. Another feature that made it distinct was its reliance on cutting-edge electronic equipment to create beats and rhythms.

Some of the earliest rock bands in the 1960s were The Beatles, The Doors, the Rolling Stones, Pink Floyd, and The Who. The reaction to rock music from mostly younger fans across the world was tremendous—the new style of music influenced the way teenagers and young people dressed, danced, and even talked.

During the 1970s, rock music exploded in popularity and further divided into subcategories like punk rock and heavy metal. One of Anna's favorite bands was the Rolling Stones, and she was especially an admirer of the band's guitarist Keith Richards. Richards, who hails from England, founded the Stones, along with lead singer Mick Jagger. A songwriter as well

Rock music and the lifestyle surrounding it have been major influences on Anna Sui. She was particularly fascinated by Keith Richards, the guitarist for the Rolling Stones, and his girlfriend in the 1960s and 1970s, Anita Pallenberg. Here, Richards and Pallenberg are shown at a party in May 1967 at the Cannes Film Festival in France.

as a musician, Richards is acknowledged as among the best and most innovative guitar players of all time.

Anna, always the student of history, was fascinated by Richards's life story, from his humble beginnings to his budding friendship with Jagger and the other founding members of the band. She was especially interested in his longtime relationship with Italian-born actress Anita Pallenberg. Richards and Pallenberg were involved with one another, though they never married, from 1967 to 1979, and they had three children together (the youngest of whom died in infancy). In the mid- to late 1970s, Pallenberg and Richards were one of the world's premier celebrity couples, making headlines wherever they went and whatever they did. Their lifestyle was fast-paced and notorious; they were caught in possession of heroin, for example, in Toronto, Canada, in 1977 and arrested.

Their relationship epitomized the rock lifestyle in general: It was filled with excitement and even danger, and socially, it broke through all the norms of acceptable behavior. This aspect of it attracted Anna, and it influenced her vision of fashion design: She liked clothing that had a rock-'n'-roll "bad girl" look to it. (In terms of men's fashions, Sui has said, "I always like my men to look like Keith Richards.")

By the time she was 17, Anna knew that she wanted to pursue fashion more seriously. She decided to take a risk.

3

A Student of Fashion

Anna Sui had big dreams of becoming a fashion designer but no real course or path to follow to that dream. Making a splash in the fashion world did not seem feasible from where she lived, in Dearborn, Michigan. The only splash she had made so far was among her classmates at school, who admired the quirky, fun way that she dressed.

Then, she came across what seemed like an answer.

She was reading *Life* magazine and happened upon an article about two young women who also had dreams of becoming fashion designers. They attended the Parsons School of Design in New York City, where they were able to meet and network with important people in the industry. In the end, success was theirs, as they moved to Paris—arguably the fashion capital of the world—and opened their own boutique. Their sponsors in the endeavor were movie stars Elizabeth Taylor and Richard Burton.

To Anna, it seemed simple: Parsons was the place to go, and she would make the needed connections, as these two young women had done. "All she had to do was go to Parsons, thought Sui, and the rest would fall into place," one article, "Sui Generis," said. Little did she know that it would not be such a straightforward path to success. For example, one of the young women in the *Life* article was related to Irving Penn, the fashion photographer, but Anna did not know this. "As a kid," she later said, "you don't realize the connections"

FAMOUS PARSONS ALUMNI

Anna Sui is hardly the only person who attended Parsons to make a big name for herself in the fashion business. Given Parsons's reputation as the leading school in the design industry, the list of distinguished alumni is long. The names include:

- **Bill Blass: William Ralph Blass was born in 1922 in a fashion household—his mother was a dressmaker. After graduating from Parsons, he entered the military. His design business was launched in 1970 and was successful from the start because of his classy, sophisticated, finely tailored looks.**
- **Marc Jacobs: Jacobs, who is Sui's friend and one of her favorite designers, won Parsons's Design Student of the Year award in 1984 while he studied at the prestigious institute. A New York native, Jacobs is the youngest person ever to win the Council of Fashion Designers of America's Perry Ellis Award for new talent.**
- **Donna Karan: Karan, whose father was a tailor and mother a fashion model, launched her design business in 1984, and her DKNY (Donna Karan New York) label is successful internationally. She created the seven-piece concept, a wardrobe composed of seven interchangeable clothing items that work well together and that can take the wearer from work to an evening out to a more casual setting. Parsons awarded her an honorary doctorate in 2004.**

that people have; it is easy to imagine that success just happens overnight.

Despite her naïveté about how the world of fashion operated, the *Life* article nevertheless showed her an open door. After all, to stay in Dearborn was not going to help launch her fashion career; she had to relocate to the place where fashion trends were established, not followed. She had to go where

- **Isaac Mizrahi: A native of Brooklyn, New York, Mizrahi is as famous for his personality as for his fashion. He has had his own show on the Style network and regularly appears in films and other television programs. In 1989 and 1991, the CFDA awarded him its Womenswear Designer of the Year prize.**
- **Narciso Rodriguez: Born in 1961 to Cuban immigrant parents, Rodriguez defied their hopes and expectations when he decided to pursue a fashion career rather than be a doctor or a lawyer. However, he would eventually make them proud with the success of his designs. After attending Parsons, he worked at several fashion companies, such as Anne Klein, until he had a major break: His friend, Carolyn Bessette, wore a wedding gown of his design when she married John F. Kennedy Jr. The dress, like the wedding, received a lot of media attention, and Rodriguez's designs were suddenly in high demand. He has also designed outfits for first lady Michelle Obama.**
- **Behnaz Sarafpour: A former employee of Mizrahi's design house, Sarafpour is a newcomer to the fashion scene, launching her label in 2001. At Parsons, she won the Golden Thimble Award for her designs. She regularly highlights organic fabrics in her shows as part of her dedication to environmental issues.**

To fulfill her dream of becoming a fashion designer, Anna Sui decided to attend the Parsons School of Design in Manhattan. Many famous designers have gone to Parsons, including Bill Blass, Donna Karan, and Isaac Mizrahi. Another Parsons alumni, Behnaz Sarafpour *(above)*, launched her clothing line in 2001.

the action was if she were to have any chance to realize her dream.

The Parsons School is part of The New School and a member of the Association of Independent Colleges of Art and Design, an organization of the leading art schools in the nation. Located in Greenwich Village, a hub of culture in the city, the school was founded in 1896 as the Chase School by impressionist painter William Merritt Chase. It was originally located in Sutton Place, in Midtown Manhattan, and it underwent several name changes over the years, as its mission developed, matured, and changed as well. In the early 1900s, for example, it was renamed the New York School of Fine and Applied Art because of the addition of a new arts curriculum that included interior and graphic design. It has been, since then, the most cutting-edge arts school in the country, as it has been able to incorporate whatever was happening in the arts scene directly in the classroom.

The school's reputation as the leading arts school was cemented by Frank Alvah Parsons, who joined as a faculty member in 1904; in 1911, he became the school's director, a position he held until his death in 1930. He helped guide the school to stay on top of developments in the art and fashion industries. The United States was reaping the success of the Industrial Revolution, and Parsons saw that art would play a major role in American industry; design would be a part of most items produced and manufactured in the country, from garments to home décor to furniture to buildings.

Parsons was responsible for establishing the school's fashion design department, which was initially focused on costume design but later became more specialized and focused on everyday garments. With Parsons's emphasis on practicality and the business of fashion as well as the creativity of it, the department developed quickly into one in which students were taught to sketch designs and cut and sew garments for sale to retailers. It was the first fashion design department in the nation and was emulated and copied by other schools.

Parsons also helped support a program in which leading fashion designers were invited to teach courses at the school and come to the classroom as guests to comment on the design work of students. The school's name was changed yet again to the Parsons School of Design in 1939 in honor of its innovative director.

Part of Parsons's success as a school and model for fashion and design education lies in its mission: "By locating visual beauty in the ordinary things of middle-class American life, Parsons virtually invented the modern concept of design in America. From the beginning, the faculty cared about the spaces people lived in, the garments they wore, the advertising they read, the furniture and tableware they used." The school focused on making the everyday items people used beautiful, aesthetic objects. During the 1960s, when social norms were being questioned and uprooted on every level (as a result of the Vietnam War, the civil-rights movement, the women's movement, and other social issues), the Parsons School demonstrated its ability to adapt rapidly to the realities of the times; for example, its Interior Design Department, which used to focus on upper-class home design, began to look at design issues related to schools, prisons, urban homes, and low-income housing.

This was in keeping with the school's mission that art and design should be democratic and accessible to all people, not just the wealthy segments of society.

MOVING TO NEW YORK CITY

It is not by coincidence that Parsons, as well as many other leading design schools, was established in New York City.

The history of New York as America's fashion capital is based on economics. By the time of the Industrial Revolution in the late 1800s, machines and manufacturing had made it easier and faster to produce clothing. Before that, fashion designers had worked almost exclusively for wealthy clients because most clothes had to be tailored to each person's individual figure. The speed at which clothing could now be produced, however, led to a demand for prêt-à-porter apparel, or clothing that was ready to wear off the clothes hanger and did not need to be fitted to an individual's body shape. As demand increased for this clothing, which was less expensive and therefore more appealing, so did the need for people to work in the garment industry. Jobs were created, and the now historic Garment Center, located around Seventh Avenue in New York City, grew quickly and employed thousands of people.

As a result, fashion houses flocked to the city as well, establishing their headquarters and flagship stores there, because they could find the best fabrics and get clothes produced very quickly. To this day, New York ranks with Paris and Milan, Italy, as one of the world's fashion centers, where design careers are made. New York's famous "Fashion Week" sees hundreds of fashion shows staged in the city every year, debuting new designers and showcasing the latest work of more established artists.

Anna knew she had to get to New York City, somehow.

She applied to Parsons, to the initial dismay of her parents. They eventually realized, however, that their daughter was determined to succeed, and so they decided to support her dream and help her as much as they could. Their change of heart may possibly have been helped by the fact that, before the end of her senior year in high school, Anna had not only been accepted to Parsons, but she received a scholarship to attend as well.

New York City is overwhelming to most people; after all, with a daytime population of 8 million people, it is the most crowded city in the United States. Greenwich Village, where Parsons is located, was a historic cultural hub on the lower west side of Manhattan, filled with art studios, museums, clubs, and other attractions. For a young woman who was barely 18 years old and had grown up in the suburbs of the "Motor City," it was an amazing experience. Anna wanted to try all the new possibilities the city offered, from going to dance clubs to attending art shows and gallery openings to eating new and different foods, attending concerts, and more. In fact, she grew tired of living in Parsons's dormitory and, after just two months there, she moved out with some roommates to a nearby apartment.

As one article puts it, her move out of the dorms "kicked off the wild years that preceded adulthood." Living on her own, with a lack of supervision, Sui became a party girl, going out almost every night with her friends and paying less and less attention to her studies. "Soon," the article "Sui Generis" added, "Sui's apartment became known as Clubhouse Central. People made a routine of meeting at her place each evening before venturing out. They partied, dressed up, took pictures." Sui's life was focused on having a good time, meeting new people, and experiencing all the city had to offer.

Part of the party scene included experimenting with drugs. In "Sui Generis," she said, "I never liked getting high. . . . I've seen too many lives destroyed." Despite having used drugs, she added, "I'm totally against drugs now." In fact, she has been saddened to see that some of her friends from those days have suffered through years of addiction and ruined their lives.

Yet, Sui says, the 1970s was a "very permissive era," and she believes that "you are a product of your time." Living in New York City, she believes, an innocent, wide-eyed teenager from Michigan could not help but immerse herself in the wild action that surrounded her.

During those years, Sui formed a network of colleagues and friends with whom she is still very close and who would later help her in her career goals. One person she befriended was Steven Meisel, who was also a student at Parsons. Like Sui, Meisel was born in the mid-1950s and displayed an early interest in fashion. Rather than play with toys as a child or show an interest in things his friends did as an adolescent, Meisel spent his time sketching. He especially liked to sketch pictures of glamorous women in haute couture, relying upon photographs and illustrations in fashion magazines to inspire him. He pored over issues of *Vogue* and other periodicals to glean ideas for his own drawings.

Meisel followed the careers of famous models, such as Twiggy (the celebrity name of Lesley Hornby), who revolutionized the fashion world in the 1960s with her ultra-slim frame and short, androgynous hairstyle. Most models before

Anna Sui hung out at the Marc Jacobs fashion show in April 1997 with James Iha *(left)*, guitarist for The Smashing Pumpkins, and fashion photographer Steven Meisel. Sui and Meisel met in the 1970s while they were students at the Parsons School of Design. The two remain close friends, and Meisel has played an important part in furthering Sui's career.

that time were admired for their curves and feminine looks, while Twiggy was quite thin and boyish in her appearance. Meisel was fascinated by how Twiggy had made such an impact on the world of fashion, with designers rushing to craft garments suited to this new, completely different female figure. Other models whom he idolized hailed from the same time period and had the same "look" as Twiggy, such as Jean Shrimpton.

Meisel had attended the High School of Art and Design, which was founded in 1936 in New York City and is considered a premier academic institution for talented teenagers who want to pursue the arts as a career. By then, Meisel was sure that design was in his future, and he had demonstrated a keen insight into and innovative perspective on the art scene.

He and Sui became good friends, spending a lot of time together and learning from each other. What they also had in common was that school had become boring to them. They found more to learn from and to inspire them on the streets of New York City. "If I did [study], I got an A," Sui said of her Parsons classes. This sentiment was a complete turnaround from two years earlier, when she was a young girl in Michigan eager to get to America's fashion capital. It seemed now that Parsons had just been a way to get to the city, not to make her career in and of itself.

Sui never graduated from Parsons. Instead she left the school after two years of course work. In discussing her surprising decision (after all, she left Michigan for New York to attend Parsons), and in reflecting on formal fashion education, Sui said in a 2005 article:

> Most of the actual things you need to know are not taught in schools; you learn these things on your first job. That is why it is often a good idea to get an internship at a company while still in school (often unpaid,

> but great experience and good for your résumé). There are many ways to become (or to be) a fashion designer. Designers work in all sorts of ways; some don't even know how to draw at all (though, the more you develop your skills the easier it is to express your ideas to others).

What is clear is that, by 1975, she had stopped taking classes and began to work.

4

The Big Launch

A classmate had told Anna Sui that the Charlie's Girls company, owned by Erica Elias, was hiring. Sui applied and was hired on the spot. She spent 18 months with the company, learning the major and most minor details of the fashion industry.

By 1981, due to her good luck in being featured in a Macy's advertisement, Sui had launched her own small clothing line. She enjoyed tremendous support from her friends during those early years in which she struggled. Steven Meisel, who had cemented a reputation as a fashion photographer, hired her for small jobs as a stylist on his shoots. By this time, he was working for *Lei* magazine, an Italian fashion journal. He invited her to join him on his travels, as cited in "Sui Generis," saying, "Why don't you bring a suitcase of your stuff and play?" Stylists for photo shoots are responsible for putting together the "look" of the shoot by assembling the clothing and accessories the models wear in the photographs.

According to one article, "Sui's professionalism prevented her from taking advantage of these opportunities to showcase her own designs. Styling one or two stories a month was a big help financially." Other friends also found her some freelance jobs, and she was grateful for the money. Sometimes she also called her parents and asked for financial help, and they did come through for her.

"My biggest problem was always money," Sui recalled in her *Newsweek* essay. "Starting with $300 is not a good business plan. I had to do extra design jobs to keep my company going for the first 10 years. I reinvested every penny I made back into the business. There were times when I didn't even have enough money for a subway token." She added, "You have to have incredible focus [to succeed]."

Meisel also did photography work for *Vogue* in Italy, and the magazine offered Sui a job as a fashion editor at one point. However, she did not like the idea of working for someone else again. She feared it would compromise her own initiative and eventually cause her to close her business, despite all the years of hard work she had invested.

A BIG MOMENT

Her business grew steadily, though she still lacked her "big moment"—a chance to introduce her clothing line on a broader scale to the fashion world. She did, however, make major steps in advancing her line. Two years into being on her own, she borrowed $30,000 from the bank; within six months, she had paid off the entire amount. This was a big accomplishment for someone with a fledgling business, and Sui was proud of herself. "I always paid all my bills," she said contentedly in "Sui Generis," "although it hasn't always been easy."

Another step included moving her work space. According to one article, "For the first [several] years, Sui's business was run out of her apartment, which was notorious for its leopard-skin carpets and purple dining room, with boxes piled to the

(continues on page 38)

Between the Generations

DISCRIMINATION, THEN ASSIMILATION

Chinese immigration to the United States can be viewed in three phases: 1849–1882, 1882–1965, and 1965 to the present.

The first wave of Chinese arrived on U.S. shores in the mid-1800s. They were mostly illiterate young men from Chinese villages, who worked as laborers in mining and manufacturing during the Gold Rush boom in the West. The Chinese also helped in the building of the transcontinental railroad. When the Gold Rush ended, Americans were suddenly unsatisfied with the high number of Chinese within their borders, and the Chinese Exclusion Act of 1882 was passed, restricting immigrants from China.

From 1882 to 1965, the few Chinese permitted entrance to the United States were wealthy or had governmental or diplomatic connections. Others who had jobs as professionals, such as academics or business owners, were allowed to enter, as well.

By 1965, the civil-rights movement, prompted by the call for equality on the part of African Americans, was a dominant political force in the United States. The 1882 Chinese Exclusion Act was reversed, and the number of Chinese entering the United States increased vastly. Many were either seeking better jobs or were fleeing the political and financial problems of their home country.

Whichever wave ushered in Chinese immigrants before 1965, their treatment in the United States was typically the same: Chinese Americans had few rights, a plight shared by many other ethnic and religious minorities at one point or another, such as Jews, Irish, Italians, and Latinos, not to mention the long-suffering African-American population.

The U.S. legal system usually made it difficult for Chinese Americans to protest discrimination, and many struggled to learn English and were thus locked out of the system from the start. Chinese immigrants were also especially susceptible to discrimination because they looked "foreign" to Americans, unlike members of other groups who could "pass" for being a white American, simply by changing an ethnic last name.

One major form of discrimination was in the housing sector. Before 1965, when they became quaint tourist attractions, Chinatowns were usually ghettos in which Chinese immigrants were forced to live, since few neighborhoods welcomed them.

The result of such anti-Chinese sentiment and hostility was that the Chinese community generally folded into itself. Since assimilation into American culture seemed so improbable, the Chinese worked on preserving their own traditions and culture. Many also arrived in the United States with the goal of earning enough money to eventually return to China. Naturalization and citizenship were regularly denied to Chinese immigrants before 1965, making this goal an understandable and realistic one.

The civil-rights movement in the United States, and the resulting end of legal discrimination against the Chinese, has made the country a more welcoming place for post-1965 immigrants. Many new arrivals to the United States find established support centers awaiting them, such as services to learn English, find work, and enroll in schools. Many of these services are, of course, provided by Chinese grassroots organizations, but many are also part of governmental initiatives. In recent decades, the Chinese community has, likewise, become more assimilated to American culture, and many Chinese Americans have entrenched themselves and risen to the top of American businesses, academic institutions, and industries. Some of them, like Anna Sui, have even felt that they are as much Chinese as they are American—a true success story.

(continued from page 35)
ceiling." One morning, in 1987, she remembers, she woke up in her apartment, opened her bedroom door, and was confronted by the sight of boxes, clothing racks, and fabric rolls stuffed in her living room. She had been living this way, with her apartment as the makeshift quarters of her business, for too long, and she decided that morning to make a change.

She moved her line into the Annett B. Showroom, a private showroom owned and managed by Annette Breindel (who dropped the "e" from "Annette" when naming her showroom because it made for a better business card). Breindel was a merchandiser who had a reputation for helping new designers establish their clothing lines and sell their garments. Sui called up Breindel and said, "My rep thinks I should talk to you," then went in with her portfolio of clothing she had designed. Breindel, however, explained a long-standing rule to the eager young Sui: "I won't talk to you unless you bring me your clothes." Breindel, who had been in the business for years, preferred to see the clothing in person, rather than just look at pictures of clothes.

Sui returned with some of her clothes, and Breindel was impressed. "After I saw her clothes, I flipped out," she recalled in a *WWD* article. "She was extraordinarily talented."

Breindel helped Sui learn aspects of the business that she had not understood earlier. For example, she advised Sui to focus on designing dresses. "Annette helped me enormously," Sui said on FashionEncyclopedia.com. "She helped me build my dress business first because that's what she saw as a worthwhile area." Breindel also advised her to focus on how her clothes fit the consumer, recalling that there had been complaints about Sui's clothes: They looked good, but they did not sit well on the average woman's figure. Breindel suggested some improvements and also advised Sui to design a line of vests and fitted pants. Sui did, and the line was a hit. "That was probably the best group she's ever done," Breindel said in *WWD*. "She sold more than she'd ever sold. That started her on a roll. She really trusted my input."

Around this time, Sui also rented out a loft in the Garment District and moved her work space there. It allowed her easy access to the resources of the historic district and gave her more living space in her own apartment, which had been packed to the hilt with boxes and racks.

Meisel also helped Sui by introducing her to the models and celebrities he had met through his photography work. In 1990, when she had been working on her business for almost a decade, Sui attended a Jean-Paul Gaultier fashion show in Paris with Meisel. It was Sui's first time in Paris, and she was thrilled. To add to her excitement, they were accompanied to the show by none other than the music star Madonna. In the *Daily News*, Sui recounted what happened when they got to the show:

> She [Madonna] had a coat on when we picked her up at the hotel and she said, "Anna, I've got a surprise for you," and she took her coat off and she had my dress on. I was just, like, "Oh my God!" We'd just come from her room, and there was loot everywhere, shopping bags from Chanel. Everyone was throwing clothes at her and here she was, wearing my dress! It was such a big thrill.

The dress Madonna wore that night was one of Sui's signature baby-doll dresses, constructed of black chiffon with a low-cut back and a bow. Photographers shot pictures of Madonna, who had borrowed Sui's bracelet to complete the look, after the Gaultier show. To say the least, having the world's most famous

Wearing an orange organza floral tree print dress and a fuchsia T-shirt, Naomi Campbell walked the runway during the presentation of Anna Sui's Spring 2004 collection. Campbell and fellow supermodels Linda Evangelista and Christy Turlington appeared in Sui's first runway show in 1991, creating plenty of buzz for the designer's debut.

pop princess enthusiastically wear her clothes was excellent advertising for Sui.

The event made Sui think that she should make a bigger splash in the fashion world by staging her own show. "Later, I decided that if she liked my clothes, then maybe I was OK. That gave me the confidence to do my first runway show in 1991," Sui recalled in *InStyle*.

A runway show would be a way to introduce her clothing line more emphatically to New York and the rest of the industry. With her usual determination, Sui got to work.

SUCCESS!

Sui focused on putting on her first runway show. The problem was that she needed money to hire models and to pay other expenses—and she had none.

Again, her friends came through for her. Meisel had introduced her to several top "supermodels," like Linda Evangelista, Christy Turlington, and Naomi Campbell, all of whom loved her clothing and designs. They agreed to walk in the show and to be paid in Anna Sui dresses rather than charge a fee. Furthermore, they helped recruit several other models to appear in the show. Another friend, Paul Cavaco, was a public-relations expert and fashion editor, and he helped Sui publicize the event, which was to take place during Fashion Week in New York.

Sui focused on making the show not just a parade of clothes, but an entertainment event as well. "Influenced by the shows of Thierry Mugler and Jean-Paul Gaultier," says FashionEncyclopedia.com, "the designer created a showing that was as much about music and theater as about clothing."

Sui also worked very hard on perfecting the clothes that would be featured in the show. She designed a "head to toe" look (for which she is still revered), in which everything on

NEW YORK FASHION WEEK

New York Fashion Week is one of a handful of major events that takes place every year in the fashion industry. Typically, there is a spring event as well as a fall event, during which hundreds of designers—both established and emerging ones–display their newest and latest fashions.

The conception of New York Fashion Week is a direct result of world history, specifically, that of World War II. In 1943, the war was raging in Europe, and the French fashion industry—then the world leader in fashion—was crippled. People from the United States—designers, media representatives, and others—could not travel to attend fashion events in Paris, so fashion publicist Eleanor Lambert put on a show to feature American designs.

According to writer Amanda Fortini, "Lambert was a canny PR maven who recognized that it was a propitious moment for American fashion. Before World War II, American designers were thought to be reliant on French couture for inspiration." Now, the world would have a chance to focus on the work of American designers as well.

Originally called Press Week because it was geared toward fashion editors and not buyers, the event was a success and attracted a lot of attention, especially from many of the leading fashion magazines, like *Vogue* and *Harper's Bazaar*. Fortini writes, "American styles were praised as modern, streamlined, and flattering, and American ready-to-wear designers were finally garnering the respect previously reserved for European couturiers."

For the first time, American designers were able to compete with their French counterparts, and New York was able to place itself alongside Paris and Milan as one of the world's leading cities for fashion.

the model is coordinated—for example, the shoes and the accessories complete the whole outfit (just like when she was an adolescent and would design shoes to match her new outfit for school). She designed a group of clothing that featured miniskirts, textured tights, wild hats, and formal but funky suits—and lots of bold, fun color.

The show was a success. The combination of rock and punk music, colors, and hip designs made for an exciting event that thrilled her audience. *The New York Times* claimed that her debut was "a pastiche of hip and haute styles that energized both retailers and fashion followers."

Sui had officially arrived on the New York fashion scene. Orders flooded in, and soon, she was busy putting on more shows and making plans to expand her business. In her *Newsweek* essay, she attributed the success of that initial show, "one of the giant breakthroughs of my career," to some good luck: "It was a case of being in the right place at the right time. All the Japanese stores were coming to New York looking for American designers."

Sui's success did lead to the severing of some relationships, though. Even after her clothing line became such a hit, she remained in the Annett B. Showroom, displaying and merchandising her clothes there. At the time, Breindel took in another young designer, Jill Stuart, whose clothes were making a sensation. As Breindel recalled, Sui felt threatened and did not want her clothes to compete with Stuart's in the showroom. Breindel was forced to choose.

According to Lauren DeCarlo, who interviewed Breindel at the end of her showroom career, "She [Breindel] debated at length whether to stick with Sui and have 'just one famous designer,' as she put it, or if she should do what she really believed was in her best interest." In the end, Breindel believed in supporting Stuart's career, and she decided to keep displaying Stuart's clothes in the showroom. Sui, as a result, left the Annett B. Showroom. According to Breindel, Sui never spoke to her again. "I cared about Anna and appreciated her talent, ethics, and loyalty," she said.

5

Expansion

The success of Anna Sui's debut runway show prompted her to expand her business. She had left the Annett B. Showroom by then, so she decided to open her own showroom. In 1992, shortly after her successful debut, she opened a boutique at 113 Greene Street in Manhattan's SoHo neighborhood.

Owning her own boutique was a thrill for Sui for several reasons. One was that she could finally display her clothes as she felt they should be presented to the customer, which had been an issue of contention with some department stores that carried her line. In 1992, Macy's had given Sui a 600-square-foot (56-square-meter) boutique in its flagship department store in Herald Square in Manhattan, and other stores also carried her clothing lines. However, according to "Sui Generis," "Department store buyers ponder how to categorize her designs because they don't fit any of the traditional molds. It isn't a designer collection, they fret, nor is it exactly juniors or contemporary."

"They'd ask how they should sell it," Sui said.

"I wanted to showcase my clothes the way I saw them," she added.

The boutique was distinctive from the beginning, as only a boutique designed by Sui could be. It reflected her personality and taste flawlessly: The space featured purple walls, vintage rock-'n'-roll posters, Victorian furniture, and many of Sui's flea market finds (she has likened going to flea markets, one of her favorite activities, to going to church, as it holds a religious quality for her).

Once, when the *National Post* asked her to describe the "Anna Sui lifestyle," Sui responded by describing the look and feel of her Greene Street boutique:

> I think [the Anna Sui lifestyle is] the experience you get when you walk in my boutique. OK, some people say it's like the Addams Family haunted house, but I think the people who really get it feel it's this glamorous, rock star, kind-of-vintage but very girly environment. Those are the things they connect with. It just pushes buttons in people. People want to buy the furniture from my store; they want to know what paint color is on the wall; they want to know how I did the floors red.

Many of Sui's friends have also commented that her apartment in Greenwich Village has a similar look: It speaks to her unique vision and reflects her interests. For example, because she loved the book *The Lion, the Witch and the Wardrobe* by C.S. Lewis as a young child, she wanted to re-create part of that memory in her apartment. As a result, she took an armoire and cut out the back, and it now stands as the entrance to her walk-in closet. (Her closet also features a stained-glass window and several of the papier-mâché dolly heads that she collects.)

Sui continued to put on more shows, and her runway shows every spring and fall became anticipated events because they were entertaining and visually stunning. About her tendency to focus on music as much as clothing for her shows, Sui said in *InStyle*: "When I do a show, I don't want to just present clothes. You can come to my showroom for that. No, my attitude is 'Let's put on a show!' with music and a cool backdrop and great girls having a good time. I want everyone watching to have a good time."

Soon, Sui developed a reputation in the fashion industry as one of its most fun, hip, and original designers. An *InStyle* article once described her in the following way:

> If we were lucky enough to have five more of her in the fashion industry, the clothing business would be a lot more fun. In fact, there have been seasons when it seemed as if Sui were the only designer having a good time. But then, she retains something other far more celebrated designers have relinquished of late—freedom.

The high praise arrived from many sources as Sui's career flourished in the early 1990s. In 1993, she won the Perry Ellis Award for new fashion talent, sponsored by the Council of Fashion Designers of America (CFDA), a professional association of 300 of the foremost fashion designers in the United States. Its mission is to promote American fashion as an integral part of American culture and art. The award cemented what everyone already understood—that Sui had become one of the most important and innovative fashion designers at that point in time.

Her future was bright. She turned to her family for help as her business began to grow. Before long, she had recruited her family members, especially her father and brother, to work in her business, helping her assemble what would become a small fashion empire. "Her brother Eddy spends a lot of time at the Sunset Boulevard store," according to the

Anna Sui began to receive accolades soon after her debut runway show. In 1993, the Council of Fashion Designers of America presented Sui with its Perry Ellis Award for new talent. Here, Sui, holding the award, poses with supermodel Linda Evangelista after the ceremony.

article "Sui Generis," while "her father helps negotiate contracts and terms."

NEW FRONTIERS BEYOND FASHION

Sui once said that she had both a creative and a business side to her personality, gleaned from her artist mother and her engineer father, respectively. She applied her business side to her fashion line in the mid-1990s to expand her unique look beyond clothing.

In 1997, she launched Anna Sui Shoes during her fall runway show, which featured her "Goth" collection. The shoes, made of fine leather, were manufactured by Ballin, an Italian luxury-design company. She designed casual daywear shoes as well as more formal evening-wear styles, all with the signature Sui look.

The designs were inspired, as usual, by Sui's eclectic tastes and interests in rock 'n' roll and the 1960s and 1970s. She was also inspired by designs she had uncovered during her regular flea-market hunts, as well as her personal shoe collection, which features more than 500 pairs. For example, she paired colorful patchwork suede into a tall boot, or snakeskin into a high-heeled sandal to be worn with fishnet mini-socks—all meant to complement her clothing designs that season.

Since the successful launch of Anna Sui Shoes, she has continued to work with Ballin to create new shoes for her clothing line every year.

1997 continued to be a year of tremendous growth for Sui. It turned out that she had a vast following for her designs in Asian countries—in fact, she is one of the rare Asian-American designers to be a hit in her native country as well as the region of her ethnic origin. Fashion critic Suzy Menkes wrote in 2008 that Sui has been "the most successful Asian-American designer in terms of building a brand in the Far East. Her dark, droll

(continues on page 52)

Other Notable Individuals

FASHION STATEMENTS

Although it is not common to see Asian-American names in fashion, Anna Sui is certainly not the only person of Asian ancestry to make a splash with her style. In January 2009, for example, Jason Wu made headlines when first lady Michelle Obama wore his single-strap, white evening gown to the series of inaugural balls held on the night of her husband's swearing-in as the forty-fourth U.S. president. Born in Taiwan, Wu grew up in Canada before moving to the United States and attending the Parsons School of Design in New York. A newcomer to the fashion industry who is only in his mid-20s, Wu debuted his launch collection in 2006. (He had previously designed dolls and toys for several years.) In 2008, he won the Fashion Group International's Rising Star prize and was nominated for the Vogue Fashion Fund awards. He is based in Manhattan, where the attention from Obama's choice of inaugural gowns has heightened his profile even further.

The winner of the 2008 Vogue Fashion Fund award was not Wu, but another Asian American: Alexander Wang, who is also in his mid-20s. He grew up in San Francisco and moved to New York to attend Parsons, like Wu and Sui, but he left the school after one year. He interned at *Teen Vogue* magazine, where he learned many of the ins and outs of the industry before launching his clothing line. His clothing and designs were a hit almost immediately. Naomi Nevitt says of his signature look, "Having expanded his line to include a full range of ready-to-wear pieces, from distressed boyfriend jeans and shrunken vests to, of course, covetable cozy cardigans, Wang has continued to make a name for himself with his signature 'model-off-duty' style."

Another famous Wang in the fashion business is the reigning queen of glamorous style, Vera Wang, who is one of the best-known and most highly respected American designers. Born in 1949 to affluent Chinese-American parents, Wang spent a lot of time in Paris

because of her father's business. Her mother took her to many of the Parisian fashion shows, exposing her early to the industry and the latest trends and styles. Wang attended university in Paris as well, before completing a degree in art history at Sarah Lawrence College. For several years, she worked at *Vogue* magazine as a senior fashion editor before launching her own clothing line. Known for her wedding dress designs, which are sought after by celebrity brides like Jennifer Lopez, Uma Thurman, and Jennifer Garner, Wang has developed a reputation for an elegant, classy signature look. She avoids a trendy, modern look but also avoids very traditional styles, preferring subtle beauty in gowns and clothing that are made of the finest fabrics and feature tremendous detail, as in the embroidery and beadwork. According to Suzy Menkes, Wang "built an empire on Western wedding dresses."

Like Sui, Wang has expanded her name brand beyond fashion; she launched her signature fragrance, Vera Wang, as well as Vera Wang Princess (a best seller) and Vera Wang Sheer Veil, and a beauty and cosmetics line. She also has an agreement with Kohl's stores to design a houseware and linen collection.

Mary Ping is another young designer making her name known in Manhattan's fashion circles. Born in New York in 1978, Ping attended Vassar College; during her college years, she designed costumes for the drama department and also worked for some well-known New York designers, including Sui. Like Vera Wang, Ping is focused on the elegance of her designs, wanting each one to have its own beauty. Her biography on the Asia Society Web site notes, "An involved designer and natural multi-tasker, Ping personally works on each detail from fabric selection, draping, and patternmaking to complete show production, product identity, and branding."

(continued from page 49)
dolly-girl style, founded on a kooky 1960s London look, started in the 1980s and is now on sale across China."

In May 1997, Sui opened a boutique in Tokyo, modeled after the Greene Street store. That fall, she followed with a second boutique in Osaka, Japan's third-largest city. She also worked out a deal with Isetan, a major Japanese department store, which handles the sales and distribution of her clothing line in Japan. Working with Isetan "has been the most amazing partnership," she wrote in *Newsweek*. "It opened free-standing Anna Sui boutiques in Japan."

That year, Sui also signed an agreement with the Wella AG company of Germany to create her own Anna Sui fragrance. She was especially excited about the fragrance deal, because she considers scents to be yet another inspiration to her designs and her creations.

The deal, however, did not stop with the fragrance. Sui and Wella, which is now part of Procter & Gamble, also brought the Japanese company Albion into the deal. Albion is a major manufacturer of cosmetics and skin-care products, and the idea was to launch an Anna Sui cosmetics line as well. The agreement with Wella is "what made me a global brand," Sui said.

The signature fragrance, Anna Sui, as well as the cosmetics line, Anna Sui Beauty, debuted in 1999. The cosmetics line featured all makeup essentials, including base, liner, and eye, lip, and nail colors. "I was able to explore while I was creating it," she said of the development of the line, "adding anything that struck my fancy. The result is a collection that has all the precise colors for today's look." Some of those Sui-inspired color selections include silver, purple, gold, and blue.

In 2000, a line of skin-care products was introduced, including bath and body essentials like shampoo and conditioners, skin cleansers and lotions, and even moisture mists.

Even the packaging for the cosmetics and skin-care products could not escape being designed with Sui's distinctive look: Many of the product cases are collector's items, featuring a high level of detail.

Sui says that she develops colors and palettes that she herself loves, making the makeup collection very personal. For example, the tea rose, her favorite scent, "is infused into all her cosmetics," *Cosmetics* magazine said. Many of the eye color palettes are embossed with the rose design, and the makeup packaging is decorated with the rose theme as well.

She also chooses colors that personally excite her. "I couldn't find the right purple polish," she once said, "so I designed a whole line. Live it up, girls!" In Asia, Anna Sui Beauty products are among the top-five best sellers, while celebrities who love her products include Cher, Drew Barrymore, and Christina Ricci.

Though she is Asian American, Sui never felt limited by the makeup selections available to her. "I was always able to find something that worked for my skin," she told writer Bernadette Morra. "It wasn't until the '80s when I went to Japan that I realized there's a whole beauty industry that caters to Asian women."

Still, Sui has developed a personal philosophy behind her makeup line: "Makeup had reached a point where products were by makeup artists who were into making flawless faces with utilitarian products," she explained in the same interview. "I love the concept of makeup as an accessory. I love the novelty of it."

She treats her makeup line much as she treats her clothing line: with flair, originality, and lots and lots of color. Indeed, there are seven "keywords" of Sui's beauty items—rose, butterfly, purple, red, black, glitter, and antique. Morra said of the typical consumer, "You are . . . taken with her offbeat products . . . [:] the glitter eye crème and mascara, the waterproof mascara in electric blue and red, and the fluffy purple feather makeup brush that looks like it fell off a boudoir slipper. You may also be one of the many women who lust after Sui's display counters: black lacquered antique dressing tables with built-in eye shadows." Morra added, "The products reflect the same wild child, rock 'n' roll, bad girl sensibility evident in Sui's clothing designs."

The fragrance, Anna Sui, was also distinguished by its purple box—one of Sui's favorite colors—while the bottle itself was framed with a gilded, black edge. The scent was floral as well as woodsy, blending rose, bergamot, jasmine, and water lily with amber, cedarwood, sandalwood, and tonka. The result was a flowery, very feminine scent intended for casual daily wear, and it has found many fans.

Other perfumes soon followed the Anna Sui signature fragrance. In the ensuing years, Sui launched Sui Dreams (in 2000) and Sui Love (in 2001). (Her last name is pronounced "Swee," so the names of the perfumes were a play on the word *sweet*.) Sui Dreams, which is packaged in a blue bottle shaped like a purse with a silver cap, blends vanilla and citrus scents. Sui Love, packaged in a colorful butterfly-shape bottle, mixes floral and fruity scents with a musk and vanilla base.

Global Cosmetic Industry magazine described her perfumes as fragrances that "enrich the world of prestige scents with a typically unconventional attitude that is both modern and nostalgic, conveying wit, urban edginess, and provocatively fresh ideas."

The packaging has attracted almost as much attention as the products themselves. Joanne Blain writes that Sui's newest fragrance, Flights of Fancy, launched in 2007, "is likely to inspire many Sui fanatics to do what they have done with her other products—buy one to use and another to keep."

To introduce her fragrance Dolly Girl Ooh La Love in 2004, Anna Sui made an appearance at Bloomingdale's in New York City to sign autographs. The packaging for Sui's fragrances and cosmetics are as distinctive as the products themselves. The Dolly Girl Ooh La Love bottle is shaped like a mannequin's head.

Sui claims that the packaging is intentional. Not only does she pay attention to detail (in fact, her "head-to-toe look," in which she pays as much attention to accessories as she does to the clothing, has earned her high praise), but she is also a collector. "One of the things I always collected were my favorite boxes or perfume bottles or cosmetic packages," she told Blain. "I'm obsessive that way, so I wanted to pass on that same obsession about the packaging—like the box is so beautiful that you can't throw the box away."

In 1999, Anna Sui's business continued to prosper as she opened a boutique in Los Angeles, in West Hollywood's Sunset Plaza.

Her fourth fragrance, Dolly Girl, was launched in 2003. One year later, a limited edition of the fragrance, called Dolly Girl Ooh La Love, was released in a bottle shaped like a mannequin's head. Still later, she released Dolly Girl On the Beach, Dolly Girl Lil' Starlet, and Dolly Girl Bonjour L'Amour! Her most recently released fragrances are Secret Wish Magic Romance, Flights of Fantasy, and Night of Fancy, giving her a total of 12 scents under the Anna Sui label.

6

Anna Sui's Inspirations

As a young girl growing up in Michigan, Anna Sui started her "genius files," which continue to inspire her today. Benj Ohad Seidler, who interviewed Sui in 2005, describes the importance of the files to the designer's career:

> In what the designer calls "the genius files," Sui stashes pictures mapping her thoughts. Dating from her idyllic childhood in 1960s Michigan and her college days at Parsons School of Design in New York in the heady 1970s, "the genius files" are the gloriously colored threads from which Sui wove her tapestry. The joie de vivre of Florine Stettheimer's turn-of-the-century poetry, David Bailey's photographs of swinging London, Bertolucci's politics, Visconti's romanticism and more traditional fashion references like Chanel and Poiret get mixed and matched every season to create a gesture that is entirely fresh.

Indeed, the importance of the "genius files" cannot be underestimated in terms of the influence on Sui's designs. Her clothes have often been called eclectic, which is probably because they blend so many different influences.

"I feel so lucky," Sui told Seidler, "that I am able to use whatever currently interests me in my work: movies, travel, exhibitions, music, the flea market. The research is the fun part."

And she means "research." She spends a lot of time looking into the history of certain trends and trying to understand what generated a look or inspired it in the first place. It's an essential part of making her own look feel authentic. As Seidler wrote, "It may be only Sui, Stefano Pilati, and Miuccia Prada who start their process with academic—as opposed to conceptual or commercial—thought."

Her dedication to researching her interests comes through during an interview with Dave Lackie in which she discussed her current obsession with chinoiserie. Chinoiserie is a term used to describe European interest in Chinese-like designs, in which fabrics, décor, and other items made since the seventeenth century featured imitation Chinese styles. Sui told Lackie:

> I love chinoiserie, . . . and I went to a talk about Pauline de Rothschild and that's how I discovered chinoiserie wallpaper. There is a very famous Horst photograph of her peeking in her bedroom and it has this beautiful wallpaper. The talk was in the house of a famous decorator and she had this incredible bookshelf filled with art books. So I thought, OK, I can't just ask her about all these books. So I memorized some of the titles so I could research them later. And one of the titles was this great book on chinoiserie. I just finished reading the chapter on chinoiserie during the time of Louis XVI.

There is seemingly no limit to what can spark an idea or attract Sui's interest. "Vintage clothing, music, books, movies, museums, travel—I'm inspired by it all," she said.

ROLE MODELS

For a person who is as interested in history as Sui, her role models include many historical and modern figures. Of course, some of the most influential figures in her life have been other fashion designers. Her role models in this sense include Coco Chanel, Ossie Clark, Emilio Pucci, Paul Poiret, and Zandra Rhodes. It is interesting to explore these designers and see how each one influences Sui's work.

Coco Chanel has inspired many international designers, and her influence on Sui is not a surprise. Gabrielle Bonheur Chanel was a French designer, born in 1883, whose stylish, simple, sophisticated clothing for women become her staple. Rather than focus on simple designs, however, what Sui learned from Chanel was to make well-constructed clothing from rich, quality fabrics. Also, Chanel was the first designer to produce a fragrance with her name attached to "brand" it: Chanel No. 5, one of the best-selling perfumes of all time.

Raymond "Ossie" Clark was a contemporary of Mary Quant's and helped inspire and shape the fashion of 1960s swinging London. Growing up in England, he practiced making clothing for his dolls and even for female friends, fine-tuning his tailoring skills. Not long after graduating from the Royal College of Art, he had a feature in British *Vogue* magazine, and London stores began to sell his clothes. He always found inspiration for his clothes in music, to which he was practically addicted, as well as art—he saw a connection between all three forms of expression. It is easy to see how music and art influence Sui's design work as well.

French designer Paul Poiret was born in 1879 in Paris; as a teenager, he sold sketches of his innovative, glamorous

Paul Poiret, a French fashion designer born in 1879, was known for his flowing designs. Two of his pieces–a hooped tunic with harem pants *(left)* and a tunic of gold lamé and purple silk satin–were part of the *Poiret: King of Fashion* exhibition held in 2007 at the Metropolitan Museum of Art in New York City. Poiret is one of several fashion designers whom Anna Sui admires.

designs until he built a reputation for himself as a cutting-edge fashion talent. He deliberately stayed away from the tailored, tightly fitting look that was popular during his time, opting to design dresses and clothing that allowed women more freedom of movement, such as his famous kimono dress and harem pants. After designing his own clothing line in 1903, he became an expert at branding his label: He hosted wild parties, designed eye-catching window displays, and styled bold clothing to make a name for himself. He also expanded his brand to other items, such as furniture and perfume, a marketing strategy that is popular today with many designers.

British fashion designer Zandra Rhodes began her career designing textiles that were initially considered too bold and did not sell well to manufacturers. In the late 1960s, she opened her own design and retail business, where her fashions found a warmer reception among her clientele, who later included notables like the late Princess Diana. Her clothes have been described as bold, colorful, and dramatic, but always feminine. Rhodes's own personality is as outrageous as some of her clothing: She often dyes her hair bright shades of pink, green, or blue—and sometimes several colors at once.

Born in 1914, Emilio Pucci was an Italian fashion designer whose work became synonymous with the look of the 1960s. He first became famous because of a set of skiwear he designed for women; the ski clothes had a sleek, polished look, with fitted stretch pants. The skiwear was featured in a fashion magazine, later prompting many manufacturers to request orders from Pucci. The socialite realized that what had started as a fun endeavor could become a major career with big profits. He left the military to launch his fashion company and designed scarves, swimwear, and other accessories. Known for making clothing from stretchy, sleek, tight-fitting fabric, Pucci is most famous for his bold prints, which feature colorful patterns. His prints serve as an inspiration to Sui, who relies on bold colors and designs herself.

THE DOLLY BIRD INFLUENCE

The Dolly Girl is a look—mired in the 1960s—that often comes to mind when one thinks of how to describe Sui's style.

Laura Craik wrote of Sui, "Anna Sui has always ploughed her own furrow. . . . Her heart is in the Sixties, the hippy spirit of which tends to pervade all her collections in some way or another." Sui, however, studies the era that inspires many of her designs with an attentive, serious eye.

As a teenager, Sui was interested in history, and she brings this same interest to her fashion creations. The "Dolly Girl" look has its roots in what is referred to as the "dolly bird" style of 1960s London, a time that Sui idolizes. In British slang, a "dolly bird" was a young woman, usually associated with London of this era, who was obsessed with the latest fashions and music scene.

It is a look that Sui seeks to bring back.

London in the 1960s had a reputation as a "swinging city," where rules were broken, young people revolted against the styles and norms of their parents, and fashion trends were pushed to and often beyond their social limitations. While womanhood in previous generations had been represented by the image of the mother and housewife, in the 1960s, the new look of womanhood was the single, sexy young woman—who determinedly made herself look like a little girl. As Rosie White wrote, "Across the Atlantic, the British 'dolly bird' offered a different kind of femininity. . . . She represents a disturbing, prepubescent femininity."

The London dolly bird girl was usually represented wearing miniskirts or hipster pants and often revealing shirts and tops; she was epitomized by models like Twiggy and Jean Shrimpton, whom White described as "gawkish" British girls who had

The English fashion model Twiggy *(above)*, with her thin, androgynous look, captured the image of the "dolly bird" of 1960s London. The miniskirt, espoused by designer Mary Quant, was also a symbol of the times, as it gave women more freedom of movement.

an androgynous, boyish look to them. The ultimate symbol of this generation of dolly birds was the miniskirt, which allowed women more freedom of movement as well as a visual way to assert power over their own bodies (a major change from the corsets and buttoned-up fashions of previous generations).

The look of the dolly bird probably originated in the styles and designs of Mary Quant, who opened her own boutique, Bazaar, on the King's Road in London in 1955. She had launched her business at an ideal time, when young women of London were seeking to express themselves with new, different, and fun styles. Inspired by the look of the 1920s "flapper girls," who wore scandalously short dresses, Quant began to market the miniskirt, along with colorful tights to be worn underneath. She knew right away that she had hit upon an instant success. Within 10 years, her business had expanded tremendously and a whole set of fans, known as the "Chelsea" set, flocked to her boutiques to buy her designs. She opened more boutiques and began to export her clothes to Europe and the United States to meet the high demand.

Quant was most successful in competing with the Paris couturiers by producing low-priced, affordable, ready-to-wear clothes that her young clientele could buy. Dubbed the "high priestess of Sixties fashion," Quant inspired many '60s-era designs beyond the miniskirt, such as hot pants, baby-doll dresses, and short, angular haircuts called "bobs." The style of this time is often called the Mod look, short for Modern, which implied that it was simple, original, and intended to provide freedom of movement and expression.

THE UNISEX LOOK

Mod fashion, as popularized by Quant, is one of Anna Sui's favorite looks, and one aspect she likes most about it is the unisex, androgynous style it makes possible. For example, one reason that she so admires Anita Pallenberg (the former longtime girlfriend of Rolling Stones guitarist Keith Richards) is that, as she puts it, "Anita introduced the world to unisex clothing." Sui explained in *InStyle*, "She liked to wear boys' clothes, and a lot of what Keith wore was hers, like the ruffled shirts. To this day she has truly great style."

Pallenberg has become one of Sui's good friends: "She's a muse to many fashion designers," Sui said, "including Bella Freud, Marc Jacobs, and Vivienne Westwood. She's an inspiration to me, too, and she has become a really good friend. One of my favorite things to do is see what's new in her closet."

Another rock duo that inspired Sui with their unisex look was Mick Jagger, the lead singer of the Rolling Stones, and his former girlfriend Marianne Faithfull. During the 1960s, when they were together, the two often sported the androgynous look. In discussing some photographs of Jagger wearing a dress, Sui said:

> I love Mick Jagger in this dress. It wasn't even his girlfriend Marianne Faithfull's; it was made for him. Exploring androgyny was a form of rebellion against the established image of what a man should be. Mick wore the dress to this Hyde Park concert dedicated to his bandmate Brian Jones.

Sui continues to look to rock music to inspire her designs today. In speaking of Shirley Manson, lead singer of the rock band Garbage, Sui said, "I think she looks like the ultimate rock chick, with the big eyes and eye makeup, red hair and white skin. She loves to play with fashion, and her choices are always interesting." In the *InStyle* article, Sui admired a photograph of Manson: "Like here, where she combines the rock-and-roll T-shirt with the little Mary Quant-style schoolgirl skirt. I like the irony of that. . . . Shirley's wearing a New York Dolls shirt, and they're one of my favorite bands ever." Many of Sui's own designs feature the T-shirt and miniskirt look that she admires so much.

Indeed, the New York Dolls, a popular rock band that emerged in the early 1970s, epitomizes much of what Sui says

GOING TO "CHURCH"

Anna Sui has said on numerous occasions that scouring through flea markets is her version of attending church. Writer Tim Allis adds that "her two-bedroom . . . apartment is a virtual shrine to that faith. Awash in red from floor to ceiling," he explains, "it is crammed with secondhand furniture, metal-framed mirrors, photos of '60s rock stars, and a collection of tiny dolls dressed by Dior, Chanel, and Givenchy."

New York City, home to more than 8 million people, is known for great flea markets, and Sui hunts at the largest and best ones, such as one on Sixth Avenue in Manhattan. Her interest in flea markets is, of course, generated by her fascination with all things vintage as well as the joy she takes in finding unusual items (she once bought a geisha wig for $10 at a flea market, although she never wears it—it's for inspiration only). Her boutique on Greene Street is outfitted with furniture that she found at flea markets and sales around the city, giving her store an eclectic, original, funky look.

The flea-market funkiness is now part of her signature look. Her Spring 2009 fashion collection was described in the following way: "As always, Sui manages to raise the flea-market-chic bar without overwhelming the viewer, bringing us feminine frocks with strong details for spring '09."

One item that Sui has been successful in finding at flea markets are the dolly head mannequins, often used by hair stylists for practicing or by accessorizers for displaying hats and other items. When she first opened her boutique on Greene Street, Sui and her friends made several out of papier-mâché, and she also she admires: revolutionary, original, gender-bending style. A band that helped pioneer the punk and glam rock music scene, the New York Dolls "were totally revolutionary," Sui said in *InStyle*. "The Dolls were rebelling against everything.

displayed the many others she has collected over the years. The mannequin heads, with their innocent, painted-on expressions, have been a symbol of her product line (one of the reasons why she chose the mannequin head as the bottle design for Dolly Girl perfume).

She knows some of the best vintage shops and flea markets in New York City and has said that she shops regularly for vintage clothing at places like What Comes Around Goes Around, Resurrection, Foley & Corinna, and Cherry. She also shops on eBay to find unusual items. Shopping as Anna Sui does has a method: "You have to be willing to sift through a lot of racks to find that one special piece," she said in *Cosmo Girl*. "Even if I can't wear something, I'll pick it up as inspiration for my collection."

The obsession with vintage clothing and items is a trait she admires in others as well. She once said of Courtney Love, a popular singer in the 1990s and wife of the late Nirvana lead singer Kurt Cobain:

> She's unique. . . . She wore a lot of these baby-doll dresses. She had a great collection. They were vintage from the Sixties, Seventies, some even from the Thirties and Forties. This is around the time people started really getting interested in buying vintage again, so she was kind of a pioneer.

Sui is also interested in why other designers, besides herself, explore vintage fashions to inspire their current work. "It's nothing new," she mused in *InStyle*. "When we're as scared of the future as we are now, we look back for things that once made us happy, for what we loved about life."

They were a glam rock band, but every punk band idolized them. . . . Look at the in-your-face androgyny," she noted, "like the guy wearing the halter. Maybe that top is his girlfriend Cyrinda Fox's."

The androgynous look has inspired Sui's designs, as she is famous for creating skirts for her menswear line. The Victoria and Albert Museum in London—Sui's favorite museum—held a *Men in Skirts* exhibition in 2002. The exhibition featured the work of 60 designers who had offered a new perspective on men's fashion by exploring the "skirt," a garment worn by men during various historical periods and in different cultures. Sui's rayon skirt for men was featured, along with skirts designed by Jean-Paul Gaultier, Vivienne Westwood, Burberry, and other fashion designers and houses.

"GIRLINESS"

As mentioned earlier, Sui admires the Mod dolly bird look of the 1960s London fashion scene. The 1960s Mod style, however, is not just about the androgynous look; it also includes an element of femininity to celebrate the female figure. The femininity of the hippie 1960s, of course, is not portrayed as the look of older, sophisticated women; instead, it is the look of young, almost adolescent girls (as in the Mary Quant schoolgirl skirt design), with the focus on wide-eyed innocence.

Nobody can deny that, for all her focus on rock 'n' roll, dark colors, and eccentric designs, Sui's clothing line has always had a distinct girlish look. Cathy Horyn wrote in *The New York Times* that "many young designers . . . betray a curious reluctance to make gender-specific clothes, putting women in pretty, if shapeless sacks. But the increasing popularity of breast implants and other surgical enhancements should tell them that women will, if anything, want to look even more womanly in the future." She added, "Anna Sui understands all of this, in her fashion. She sees a collection not just as design but also for what it communicates visually, and she gives femininity the full-on treatment."

The girlishness of her designs means that her clothes have always appealed to the younger set of fashion fans (or older women who want a distinct, youthful look). A description of her Spring 2009 collection offers a good example; Laura Craik noted:

> Colors were bold—purple, kingfisher blue, and emerald green—while prints were whimsical and lifted from nature, as with a bold leaf print dress or a jacket printed with outsized flowers. Fabrics included broderie anglaise, heavy silk, and linen. As always with Sui, this was a very youthful collection, with a few too many rompersuits and baby-doll dresses to sit easily with the over-35s.

Sui is proud of the girlish, youthful look of her clothing. "There's always a very feminine, girl aspect to it," she said. "There's always that ambiguity of good girl, bad girl. All those things have to go into the clothes, or it doesn't look like Anna Sui."

Sui, however, insists that fashion "doesn't really have anything to do with age—it has to do with spirit" and that her clothes appeal to both young and older people. "[I get both] that new, young customer—maybe it's her first time buying a perfume or buying a lipstick—but we also get her mom," she told Joanne Blain.

This may not ring true to many fashion reviewers, though, who see Sui's styles as distinctly for the young set. Anne-Marie Schiro wrote of Sui's 1993 runway show, which featured sheer baby-doll dresses worn over black underwear, among other things, "Anyone can buy Anna Sui's clothes, but not everyone has the style to carry them off." Alex Kuczynski wrote, "As much as I admire her, I don't like her makeup and perfume. The

With their sense of girlishness, Anna Sui's designs have always appealed to younger buyers. Here, models show off Sui's clothes from her Spring 2009 collection. "Colors were bold–purple, kingfisher blue, and emerald green–while prints were whimsical and lifted from nature," one reviewer wrote about the collection.

cosmetics are seriously vivid and a bit chalky and caky. Ms. Sui is no Bobbi Brown, no mistress of subtlety or proponent of the nude lip. When you wear her makeup, she wants you to look as if you're wearing makeup. This works if you are 18 or a rock star or are trying for a *Whatever Happened to Baby Jane?* look."

The criticism may be appropriate, given that Sui's look is often considered "cute" and "adorable"—not the way many adult women want to look. Nevertheless, it is unlikely to cause Sui to change her style or alter the sense of fantasy and fun she brings to her clothing line.

GOTH

Goth culture was an offshoot of the punk-rock scene that emerged in the late 1970s. It has associations with music, literature, and fashion, and usually takes as its inspiration Victorian culture, romantic themes, and a focus on morbidity and death. In terms of fashion, it can be characterized by an emphasis on the color black, as well as other dark hues such as purple and rich fabrics like velvet.

Sui likes the goth look, and it seems that many goth adherents like Sui's designs as well. "Anna Sui may not be a household name," wrote Dave Lackie, editor of *Cosmetics* magazine, "but to a legion of 20-something and teen girls who favor goth culture and alternative music, she's an icon." What probably appeals to these young fans is Sui's ability to make the dark and morbid also look feminine and sexy.

For example, Sui designed a collection of black jewelry that has goth undertones. The collection was inspired by jewelry made of black jet that she found at a London store in 1987. (Jet is a dense coal that can be polished and is commonly used to make jewelry.) The find in London inspired Sui to research the history of using black jet. She discovered that, in 1861, after the death of Queen Victoria's husband, the monarch wore only jewelry made of jet, because it symbolized her mourning and loss. As a result, the queen ended up establishing a fashion trend, in which black clothing and somber-toned jewelry became popular among England's couture-minded set. Black jet was used to make large, chunky jewelry with big beads and attention-getting pendants.

Upon further research, Sui discovered something that really got her excited. The best black jet, it turned out, came from the town of Whitby, in Yorkshire, England, which provides the setting for parts of Bram Stoker's famous novel, *Dracula*. Sui became obsessed with visiting Whitby.

According to Sandra Ballentine, "Seven years ago, [Sui] finally made a pilgrimage to that seaside town with her pals the style icon Anita Pallenberg and Andrew Bolton, the associate curator at the Costume Institute at the Metropolitan Museum of Art. Their trip coincided with Halloween, and the biannual Whitby Gothic Weekend."

"There were all these people in white makeup and capes wandering the streets," Sui told Ballentine. "It was amazing to look at." The goth scene benefited from Sui's research and interest in black jet; she designed a few pieces featuring black roses carved from jet, which have sold very well.

Lackie sees something in the "real psychological connection" Sui has made with the young goth crowd: "With all the multinationals and commercialism in the beauty industry, they see Anna as the real deal. And when they find something with integrity and authenticity, they are loyal. That's what is driving her business."

7

The Collections

When Anna Sui puts together a fashion collection, once every spring and fall season, she goes through an intricate process. According to the article "Sui Generis," "The 70 to 80 looks Anna Sui must design for each of her two shows a year take more time and effort than one might imagine."

For Sui, it begins with the fabric. Finding the right fabric inspires the idea for the look or vision she wants to create that season. "I see the whole collection in my mind when I see fabric," she said in "Sui Generis." "If I see one muslin, I may see four [designs]." She then takes the look of the fabric and begins to construct designs, working both formally and informally on them. Sometimes she works in her office, but other work periods involve "doing little sketches, for example, in line at a bank or while on the phone."

Once she has a series of designs, she places each into one of three categories: suits, evening wear, or casual wear. The article "Sui Generis" continued, "Hundreds of sketches have been made by the time she goes into planning for the show. During the final few weeks, she works through weekends. It's at about this stage that accessory needs become defined," and then Sui works on makeup, hats, jewelry, and shoewear needs for each outfit. She also works out music and staging at this point.

Sometimes, no matter how hard she has worked to make sure everything goes well, problems crop up. "Fabric, fit, zipper, something will go wrong," she said. "In fact, it's a miracle if nothing goes wrong."

However, since Sui's business was formally launched with her first runway show in 1991, almost everything has always gone right. Her shows are usually social events not to be missed

SOMETHING GOES WRONG

Although Anna Sui admits that something always goes wrong with every collection, from bad fits to stubborn zippers, even she could not have anticipated the disaster that befell her Spring 2006 collection. As the designs were being loaded into a truck from her showroom, to be transported to the Fashion Coterie show, there was about a half-hour when nobody was guarding the merchandise. During that time, the police reasoned, thieves broke into the truck and stole many of the items. Most of the clothes were the only ones in existence, as it was a sample collection.

Sui was, according to writer Marc Karimzadeh, "left scrambling to reproduce the samples," which her executives admitted would be "nearly impossible" to do. The loss was estimated to be "upward of seven figures," although the real loss was how to show her designs without the actual clothing items so that retailers and buyers could view what Sui had to offer that season. As Karimzadeh wrote, "The lion's share of the stolen merchandise was from Sui's February delivery, which is the first for spring and typically the designer's largest of the season."

by fashion fans, including many celebrity actors, musicians, and other notables, who adore Sui's tastes and are excited to see what she has cooked up for each season.

For Sui, the look of each season is also closely connected to a high level of research. Much of that research is historical, and it offers insights into the sources of her inspiration. Below are highlights and glimpses into some of her collections and the ideas that sparked their creation.

FALL 2004

Sui loves museums and attending exhibits, especially when those exhibits focus on fashion. In 2003, she attended one such exhibit at the Philadelphia Museum of Art on Italian fashion designer Elsa Schiaparelli. The experience, and Sui's subsequent research into Schiaparelli's work, helped guide the look of her Fall 2004 collection.

Born in Rome in 1890, Schiaparelli studied in London, where she met her husband. Later, the couple moved to New York, although the marriage failed after the birth of their daughter. Left alone to raise her child, Schiaparelli began to work for a friend who owned a fashion business, designing clothing. When the friend moved her business to Paris, Schiaparelli and her daughter followed. There, the young Italian woman immersed herself in the fashion world and was soon inspired to make her own line of clothes.

Her business had a difficult beginning, but eventually she found a following for her line, which featured sportswear for women, known as "pour le Sport." Her look was nothing other than modern and intended to be worn by the modern woman. Her knitwear was very popular and garnered the designer her first bout of high praise from the critics; for example, she designed a black pullover sweater, with a white bow knot woven into the neck area. The effect is a trick of the eye, in which the viewer thinks the wearer has a scarf wrapped around her neck.

This ensemble—featuring a pink posey border print, lace-trimmed chiffon dress; a plum multi-colored knit cardigan; and an orange silver fox collar—was part of Anna Sui's Fall 2004 collection. The Italian fashion designer Elsa Schiaparelli, known for her detail as well as her frivolity, inspired this collection.

Such a design was revolutionary—and plain fun. *Vogue* magazine called it "an artistic masterpiece."

Schiaparelli created the split skirt, which looked like today's shorts. The design caused controversy because it made women appear as if they were wearing trousers and it exposed their legs. Her sense of fashion was quite playful, and she worked closely during her career with Surrealist and Dadaist artists like Salvador Dalí to create looks that were unusual but fun. She reveled in details, often creating buttons made of unusual materials and accents. In 1934, *Time* magazine wrote that "in her crusade for sharp, dramatic line ('skyscraper silhouet') Mme Schiaparelli persecutes the button with morbid zeal, has substituted all manner of gadgets in place of it, including metal coat fasteners in the shape of dollar signs." She enjoyed experimenting with different fabrics besides the standard cottons and silks. She once designed a cape made from heavy plastic meant to look like glass, and she also incorporated other manmade materials into her clothing, even making dresses out of rubber and collars out of china.

Time said of Schiaparelli: "Madder and more original than most of her contemporaries, Mme Schiaparelli is the one to whom the word 'genius' is applied most often. Even to her intimate friends she remains an enigma." It is easy to see how someone like Schiaparelli instantly fascinated a designer with the same proclivities, like Anna Sui, who admires genius and rebelliousness in fashion.

Sui's Fall 2004 collection reflected her heavy attention to detail, as inspired by Schiaparelli's designs. A review on Style.com called it successful, saying, "She kept the accessories crew busy, loading each look with gold chains, wrapping leopard belts over jackets and coats, and pinning lots of brooches to lapels. It could easily have been discordant, but under Sui's guidance the result was a burst of much-needed cheerful noise."

FALL 2005

Sui said that she wanted the models in her Fall 2005 runway show to look as though they were going to a Louise Nevelson exhibit. Nevelson, an American artist of Ukrainian heritage, was part of the "assemblage art" movement, also known as the "junk art" movement, in which three-dimensional objects are made from found items; the found objects thereby create something new and aesthetically pleasing.

Another artist who has influenced Sui was David Hicks, who was a very popular interior designer in the 1960s and 1970s. Born in England in 1929, Hicks had always felt that the old-style, Victorian-era home décor, popular during the time, was too stuffy and traditional. He got his start when he redesigned his mother's home in London, a makeover that was so bold and captivating that a write-up of it appeared in a magazine. From then on, Hicks applied his signature blend of old styles with modern looks to everything from wallpaper and carpets to furniture and linens. For almost the rest of his life, his designs and styles were in high demand.

An obituary in *The New York Times* described Hicks's influence: "Mr. Hicks's heady combination of bold antiques and modern furniture set off by abstract paintings, often best deployed within an envelope of cool Georgian architecture, was the last word among movers and shakers of the 1960s."

Sui's Fall 2005 collection featured Nevelson's and Hicks's inspiration, in terms of the items used to accessorize the outfits and the fabrics she chose. On Style.com, the review said that Sui "layered a pile of chunky gold chains and a foot-high fur toque on top of an Empire-waist connect-the-dot-print dress worn with fishnets and midheel loafers. And that was just for starters. An eclectic parade of menswear fabrics, butterfly prints, and metallic lamé followed."

For her Fall 2005 collection, Anna Sui was inspired by the work of artist Louise Nevelson and interior designer David Hicks. Here is one of Sui's designs from that season's collection.

SPRING 2008

Sui's father used to enjoy listening to Busby Berkeley musicals, the look of which inspired her Spring 2008 collection.

Busby Berkeley, whose real name was William Berkeley Enos, was born in 1895 into a family of performers. He began to act at the age of 5. When World War I broke out, he joined the military, rising to the rank of lieutenant; he was responsible for drilling and training large numbers of men. This perhaps influenced his later career as a choreographer, in which he distinguished himself by using large numbers of female dancers—chorus girls—to form complex sequences and geometric shapes. When he began to use chorus girls in this way in his Broadway shows, the new, daring, and regimented style was a hit. From Broadway, Berkeley went on to make movies. His dance sequences and the number of chorus girls used to stage them became larger and larger. He also used interesting camera angles, filming overhead and bird's-eye-view shots of the patterns in which he would place the dancers.

Sui also said that her Spring 2008 look was inspired by Biba, the popular London fashion store of the 1960s and 1970s. Young women flocked to Biba because it offered, through the store and later a mail-order catalog, cutting-edge fashion designs as worn by celebrities for a fraction of the cost. (The famous Biba store logo actually inspired Sui's own logo.) The logo soon appeared on everything Biba sold (menswear, women's clothing, children's apparel, home décor, etc.), albeit in a slightly different form but similar enough to be unmistakably Biba.

The Biba success was built on the backs of other designers, like Mary Quant. Barbara Hulanicki, Biba's founder, took Quant's fashions and made them affordable for the younger set. The typical Biba "look" was based on the dolly-bird, Twiggy look—a young, very thin woman with long legs and heavily made-up eyes.

Anna Sui looked to two varied sources when putting together her Spring 2008 collection–Busby Berkeley, the choreographer and director of 1930s movie musicals, and Biba, a clothing shop from swinging '60s London. The collection combined the glitter of Berkeley's chorus girls with the heavily made-up eyes symbolic of the Biba look.

In her Spring 2008 runway show, Sui mixed the Busby Berkeley chorus girl and the Biba look to create a fresh palette of dressed-up fashion. The models wore glittery clothing with high waists, a la the Berkeley girls, and the general look was a blend of Hollywood's golden age and swinging London.

SPRING 2009

Sui's Spring 2009 collection was inspired, she says, by the work of Alexander Girard. Girard, who was born in 1907, was an American textile and fabric designer. Raised and educated in Rome, Girard had a special interest in folk and ethnic art and found ways to incorporate folk themes and patterns into his designs. He collected folk art in the form of textiles, toys, dolls, and more than 100,000 other objects from around the world. He and his wife established the Girard Foundation to manage their collection, which represented ethnic art from more than 100 countries on six continents. The collection was donated to the Museum of International Folk Art in Santa Fe, New Mexico, and many of the items can be seen in the museum's Girard Wing.

One can see ethnic influences in Girard's own design work. Girard liked to use bold color and patterns and did not worry about creating a sophisticated look—he felt that "delighting the senses" should be the designer's primary concern, according to Sam Grawe. He used colors others shied away from, such as bright oranges and greens, and he incorporated geometric patterns into many of his designs. He applied this look to everything from textiles to wallpaper to restaurant designs, even to planes (he once worked on remaking the look of Braniff Airlines).

Sui liked that theory of "delighting the senses" and applied it to her Spring 2009 collection. Girard's look was "very colorful, optimistic, and happy, which is what I'm pushing these days," Sui said, especially since economic times were so dire. Her dresses and suits had an ethnic look, with some Mexican-inspired designs, and featured bold colors and comfortable, loose fits.

8

Suited for Business

Despite the usual descriptions of Anna Sui's clothes as wild, hippie, and youthful, they continue to sell well and draw a steady stream of customers, whether from New York, Los Angeles, Milan, or Osaka. Despite her success, Sui does not take anything for granted. She knows that the fashion industry is incredibly fickle.

"What we're producing is an unnecessary thing," she said in "Sui Generis" of her clothing and product lines. "The business I'm in is like gambling because you never know what's gonna sell." She understands how fashion trends can suddenly change or another designer can dominate the market. She also admits that sometimes customers "just don't want clothes."

Sui, however, prides herself on staying on top of the latest trends and maintaining a connection between her customers and herself. She enjoys talking to her customers when she is in her boutique and getting a sense of what they are looking for. "My favorite compliment about my work," she says, "has always been finding out that a woman's husband told her she looked

Backstage, Anna Sui put the finishing touches on one of her designs before the showing of her Fall 2006 collection. Sui is usually in her office by 8:00 A.M. and works well into the evening. And during the final weeks before debuting a new collection, Sui works through the weekend as well.

beautiful in my dress. What better reason do you need to make clothes?" This personal connection helps to keep her focused on who is important in her line of business: the people who will be wearing her clothes. "I get to meet everyone from young girls who come in with their mothers to design students," she says of the days that she spends in the boutique. "I love to meet them—and I love for them to see that there actually is a person behind this brand."

Keeping in touch with her customers also helps her to understand what not to do in her designs. For a designer who is reputed to be a "wild child," Sui nevertheless understands that most consumers will not go beyond a certain comfort level.

Story of My Family

A DIFFERENT IMMIGRANT EXPERIENCE

Anna Sui has said that she relieves the stress of putting together a fashion show by taking off the day after the show to spend with her family. At the most recent New York Fashion Week, many family members sat in the front row to watch her models sport her newest creations on the runway. Her father and brother both work for her business, so she is supported by family in her career.

Sui has always said that education was important to her parents, who initially could not understand why, as a teenager, she wanted to move to New York to design clothes. They supported her aspirations, however, perhaps because her parents pursued their own dreams.

Paul Sui grew up in China but moved to France, where he graduated from the Sorbonne. He met Anna's mother, Grace, who was also a student. Grace's father was a diplomat and the family traveled, so she was acclimated and exposed to different cultures, especially Western ones. When she decided that she wanted to pursue art, her family sent her to Paris to study painting. There she married Paul Sui.

The couple moved to the United States in the 1950s. Perhaps Grace's diplomatic ties or Paul's professional status helped aid their immigration, as the United States had a racist policy in those days toward Chinese immigrants. It was not until the era of the civil-rights

"I'm a very realistic designer," she wrote in *Newsweek*. "There's a big difference between a fashion show and the product that a consumer buys. In my own store, I see what women want. I hear what they're asking for." While she does not sacrifice the creativity and fantasy of her designs, Sui nevertheless incorporates a practical aspect to her work, knowing that otherwise she will lose her consumer base.

movement that the Immigration and Nationality Act of 1965 finally abolished former U.S. policy. The Chinese Exclusion Act of 1882 had severely restricted Chinese immigration to the country. The Civil Rights Act of 1964 also legally outlawed discrimination on the basis of ethnicity against Chinese Americans and members of other minority groups.

In Dearborn, Michigan, where the Suis settled, the number of Chinese Americans was very small. In fact, Chinese immigrants in Detroit, the neighboring big city, only numbered in the few thousands in the 1950s. The Suis developed a balance in which they retained their ethnic traditions but also adapted to mainstream American culture—a task made easier since Paul and Grace had both traveled widely and lived in foreign countries before.

The Sui story is, therefore, not the typical story of Chinese immigrants to other major American cities, where the newly landed were relegated to living in the Chinatown "ghettos" and forced to work in factories and at menial jobs. The Suis lived a middle-class lifestyle and raised their children as both Chinese and American. From the way their daughter's career has developed, it looks as if they had achieved the American Dream.

Focusing on her customers' needs and desires is just one part of Sui's work ethic. Dedication and attention to detail are two others. She built her business during a period of 10 difficult years, and she is devoted to every single aspect of it. "When you own your own business, you're responsible for everything, even for things like the garbage and making sure there's enough water in the water cooler," she said in "Sui Generis."

Even today, with her business so successful (the various Anna Sui lines make about $20 million a year), Sui still works long hours. She wakes up by 6 A.M., has a simple and quick breakfast, and gets to her office by 8 A.M. She usually eats lunch in her office so she can continue to work, and she wraps up her day late in the evening. When she is putting out a new collection, she often works through the weekends during the final weeks of production. According to "Sui Generis," "Whatever free time she may have is spent watching CNN and catching up on news from the world of fashion by reading magazines." She also enjoys, of course, shopping at flea markets whenever she can as a form of both inspiration and relaxation.

REPUTATION

Sui is certainly one of America's top-rated fashion designers, and her reputation is rock solid for several reasons. One is, of course, her eclectic tastes and looks. According to Benj Ohad Seidler, "Now Sui is seen as an established doyenne of New York fashion with an established style that includes precious ethereal dresses and artful prints, styled in a way that is provoking but still accessible. Where other designers are criticized for being nostalgic and using vintage references, Sui is lauded. She was doing it before it was a trend but, more importantly, when Sui does it there's a meaning."

Another factor in her reputation is the affordability of her designs. "It means just as much to me that my mom and my cousin are excited by my clothes," she said. "It doesn't have to be expensive to be hip and cool." As Tim Allis wrote in *People*, "Sui has earned a reputation as fashion's patron saint of the recession." While many of New York's foremost designers charge upward of $1,000 for their designs, Sui's pieces usually sell for no more than $200 or $300.

"I don't think people need to spend every single penny on clothing," Sui told Allis, reflecting on her own early years as a

A model displayed a mauve mesh/tie T-shirt with a print silk chiffon skirt during Anna Sui's Spring 2001 show. That collection included nearly 60 T-shirts, highlighting one of Sui's strong suits–the affordability of her clothes. The T-shirt shown here, though, is more playful than utilitarian, and Sui laments that many designers today have lost their sense of fantasy.

struggling designer in the Big Apple. "On my first assistant-designer job in Manhattan I bought a fur coat, and that coat lived better than I did. It was in cold storage in the summer while I sweated it out in a fifth-floor walk-up."

Bloomingdale's fashion director Kal Ruttenstein has said of Sui's clothing that "she gives more fashion for the price than any other New York designer." Mary Ellen Gordon said of Sui's 2001 collection that it included "59 feminine T-shirts decorated with printed designs, fabric flowers, lace, and sequins, and [they] were as fashionable as they were affordable. Never interested in haute couture, Sui's work reflects her ongoing concern to 'continue to make these clothes accessible to the people I want wearing them.' "

THE BIG PICTURE

Having been in the fashion business for so long and rising to the top, Sui also knows the industry inside and out. She understands its trends, learning what works and what does not from every season and collection. She has also seen the fashion business, especially in New York, change drastically from the time that she was beginning her own career, after her move to the city in the 1970s. As an insightful businesswoman, Sui has a keen sense of what the industry's various problems are.

For example, she feels that many designers today have lost the element of fantasy—so essential to her work—in their own clothing lines. "Fantasy is such an important part of my fashion," she said. "Everyone wants and needs to dream. Childlike elements and adults believing in optimism are key elements of all my collections."

Part of the problem is that retail merchants no longer work in a cooperative spirit with designers. Instead, she said in *InStyle*, "Today every store has to answer to another business higher-up, whose CEO is only interested in the daily bread of fashion without realizing that you need the frosting on the cake, too." Knowing the burdens that corporate structure places on the retail-designer relationship helps her to keep her business from going down the wrong path. According to Guy Trebay, "Fashion was a radically different business when she was starting out in the 1980s." Specifically, it was "less corporate, more subject to the whims and intuitions of gifted merchants."

Sui also laments the fact that, with costs so high and corporations stressing the bottom line when pondering opportunities, department stores are less willing to take a chance on new, young, and virtually unknown designers. Costs are high for the designers as well, Sui says, so young designers have the odds stacked against them.

Perhaps this is so painful for Sui because she herself was once an unknown hopeful; she may think that, in today's climate, her career may have never taken off as smoothly as it did.

GROWING AND GROWING

In 2005, Sui expanded her flagship boutique on Greene Street in the SoHo neighborhood of New York City. Writer Marc Karimzadeh joked that "Anna Sui is living larger these days," a reference to the size of the new store. Originally 947 square feet (88 square meters), the new boutique is nearly double in size, at 1,875 square feet (174 square meters).

"We were so crowded and so cramped, and everything was piled on top of everything else," Sui said of the need for the expansion.

Some things have remained the same in the new boutique, including the red floors, flea market furniture, and rock-'n'-roll posters on the walls. What is different is that room has been made to accommodate Sui's cosmetics and accessories, as well as a menswear line. What is also new is Sui's decision to sell many of the vintage clothing pieces from her archives: "Sui has used many of these pieces as inspiration for collections, and she is now ready to part with some of the coats, suits, and dresses. Each piece comes with a personal note from Sui explaining where she found the piece," Karimzadeh wrote. The vintage clothing is displayed in a large, vintage wardrobe.

She is also developing her men's line, for which she has made some space in her new, larger boutique. "I have been also really wanting to do menswear, but it was always jammed on a rack," she told Karimzadeh. In the new space, she offers her male customers a selection of shirts, ties, polo shirts, and baseball caps.

Sui is thrilled with her new space, which was made possible when an artist, who had been using the back of the boutique for studio space, moved out. "There is still the intimacy of being in my space, but now, they [the customers] can see everything and it's not all on top of everything else," she said.

Sui's growth can certainly be attributed to her savvy business sense, which, as she says, she gets from her father, Paul Sui. She has more than 300 sales outlets in 30 countries. These include 32 independent boutiques and stores, 27 accessory boutiques, and 42 accessory specialty shops, according to her Web site (http://www.annasui.com). The global exposure of her products contributes to her impressive sales revenue. And yet, Sui continues to see more and more opportunities to expand her business.

9

New York Girl

Always with her finger on the latest trends and hot cultural items, Anna Sui recently got into the toy business. Perhaps recalling the years she spent as a child dressing up dolls and toy soldiers to recreate the Academy Award red carpet shows, Sui designed her own Barbie doll in 2006. An immediate collector's item, the doll features long, black hair and bangs and is wearing an Anna Sui-inspired outfit: denim jeans tucked into suede boots, a white blouse accented with pink floral designs, rose-tinted glasses, a 1970s-style black shawl, and a vintage Victorian choker necklace. For its Bohemian style chic, the doll was dubbed Boho Barbie and was marketed by the Mattel company.

Sui also designed a special-edition Hello Kitty doll. A popular doll ever since it was released many years ago by the Sanrio company, Hello Kitty is an adorable cartoon cat that has made a comeback among young American and Asian women. Hello Kitty stationery, dolls, makeup, toys, key chains, and hair accessories—among a multitude of other items—are best sellers.

Anna Sui designed a Barbie doll in 2006 that featured the designer's trademark look. The doll was called Boho Barbie. Sui has also created a special-edition Hello Kitty doll.

Sui saw a chance to benefit from this, and her signature Hello Kitty doll sells for $295, an instant collectible.

In 2005, Sui entered into a joint venture with the well-known Victoria's Secret women's lingerie and beauty store. Along with Cosmopolitan Cosmetics, the lingerie giant launched a new Sui fragrance, Secret Wish, as one of its private-label perfumes. "While Victoria's Secret Beauty has a few other third-party scents in its doors," Julie Naughton and Brid Costello explained, "this pairing marks the first time that Victoria's Secret Beauty has exclusively launched a fragrance that is not branded under its eponymous product line."

The perfume is classic Sui: a blend of musk and floral scents, mixed with fruits as well. The bottle, of course, is just as special as the perfume, designed with three faces and topped with a fairy on the cap.

Sui has also branched out into other forms of artistic expression. In 2004, she helped design the costumes for an anime series, *Gankutsuou: The Count of Monte Cristo.*

In 2007, Sui announced that she would be launching a new brand of clothing that would target Japanese youth, one of her biggest markets. The new brand, called Dolly Girl by Anna Sui, would be carried by and sold in Isetan department stores and almost 20 other outlets throughout Japan. The target audience, women aged 18 to 25, had, in recent years, forsaken department stores to buy their clothing in specialty shops. The new Dolly Girl brand, devised between Sui and Isetan, was "a key strategy for the nation's department stories to reach these consumers via a brand with high potential," according to Koji Hirano. The potential is, indeed, high. The sales figures for the Dolly Girl brand were projected to be $25 million by the third year. The prices were also set to be affordable for these young consumers: Blouses and pants retailed for approximately $100, while coats were in the $200 range.

Sui has even found a way to merge technology with fashion in recent years. In 2005, Samsung asked her to design a special-edition cell phone. "More and more today, technology is becoming the ultimate expression of fashion," said Tom Florio of *Vogue* magazine, which was involved in the agreement. (The advertising for the phone was featured in a special section in *Vogue.*) "It was a natural fit for us to bring Samsung together with Anna Sui." The phone, launched in February 2005, was called the Anna Sui Mobile, and it had a camera and camcorder feature. Consumers who purchased it also received a signature Anna Sui phone case and a tube of her Sui Rouge lipstick.

Anna Sui's creations have taken her beyond fashion, fragrances, and cosmetics. In 2005, she designed a cell phone for Samsung. The phone, she said, "reflects my favorite things–purple, metallic black, a butterfly, glam rock, vintage-chic, all unmistakably Anna Sui."

"The wireless phone is the most visible accessory and should be an extension of your personal style and essence," Sui said of the product, adding that the phone "reflects my favorite things—purple, metallic black, a butterfly, glam rock, vintage-chic, all unmistakably Anna Sui."

It seems that Sui's creativity—which touches upon everything from television series to perfume to toys and even technology—has few limits. Indeed, it is probably a major factor in her success that she is able to see that fashion has an application everywhere. Though she did not graduate from the Parsons School of Design, this was always a mission of the faculty at Parsons, to ensure that fashion was seen as an integral part of other industries. In building her empire, Sui is doing just that.

THE SUI LEGACY

Critics of Sui's fashion designs claim that her look is simply cute at best and kitschy at worst. Most agree, however, that Sui has had a major impact on the American fashion scene and has even helped create the major looks and trends of the 1990s and 2000s.

For example, goth became quite popular in the 1990s, and young women who wear goth clothing and adhere to the lifestyle admire Sui's designs. Also in the 1990s, musicians like Kurt Cobain and Courtney Love helped style a new look, called "grunge." Grunge, which means garbage or dirt, was antiglamour, with deconstructed clothing that was often shapeless and self-consciously not fashionable. On the music scene, grunge was also anti-pop, seeking to create alternative rock sounds. In fashion, grunge distinguished itself with a look composed of flannel shirts, ripped jeans, and an overall pretense to not caring how one looked or dressed—a "thrift shop" or "secondhand" look.

When grunge's popularity began to spread among America's youth, designers like Sui and Marc Jacobs had their fingers on the pulse of the trend. Their fashion collections in the early 1990s featured models dressed in grunge style, wearing items like wool caps and army boots. There were complaints about these collections from designers and those critics used to a more tailored and polished look from Jacobs and Sui, but the two designers knew what they were doing. Sui's baby-doll dresses, which Courtney Love—the queen of grunge—made into a fashion statement, were in high demand, and grunge enthusiasts flocked to her stores and showrooms.

In the 2000s, Sui has spearheaded the hip, youthful look that kept customers coming to her again and again for clothing inspiration. Fashion in this decade has taken many turns, but bohemian chic was back in a big way, with women's wear adopting many of the designs of the 1960s and 1970s; clothing and jewelry also featured bright, bold ethnic patterns. Colorful and expressive—that is what Sui does best, so she was once again riding on the crest of this era's fashion wave.

A GRATEFUL SUI

In her early years in fashion, Sui always hoped, but probably never imagined, that she would be as successful as she has become. Her awards as a designer include the Perry Ellis Award for new talent, earlier in her career, from the Council of Fashion Designers of America, and the CFDA's Geoffrey Beene Lifetime Achievement Award in 2009. "It's really a dream career," she said in "Sui Generis," "because everything I do is incorporated into what I do. What I see, hear, you never know when it'll affect you. This was my dream."

Her dream first became possible when she moved to New York at the age of 17 to attend Parsons School of Design. To this day, she lives in the city, in her famous apartment in Greenwich Village. She enjoys the feel of the city, from the style of people living there to the fact that she can walk almost anywhere she needs to go. The cultural, art, theater, and music scenes of the Big Apple are also important to her because they fuel ideas for her work.

Sui loves New York City, and she is fighting to preserve its fashion center. The historical Garment Center has recently been threatened by a new set of zoning laws. According to Kristen Seymour, "Zoning laws have changed the way the buildings in this area are viewed, and many landlords are hoping to turn what have been factories into luxury lofts and hotels, leaving many contractors in the industry with nowhere to go." *The New York Times* reported that the number of jobs in the

In 2008, Anna Sui launched a campaign to "Save the Garment Center," as her T-shirt said. The Garment Center is the historic hub of the fashion industry in Manhattan. Rising rents have forced out many manufacturers, as landlords hope to turn the factories into loft apartments and hotels.

Garment Center has shrunk from 250,000 in the 1950s to 20,000 in 2009.

Sui uses many contractors in the Garment Center for everything from purchasing fabrics to assembling and producing the clothing she creates. Recently, several of her contractors lost their leases because they could not afford their increasing rents. The problem is bigger than Sui and her own business needs,

THE GARMENT CENTER

Also known as the Fashion District or the Fashion Center of New York, the Garment Center has a fascinating history as one of the Big Apple's oldest neighborhoods.

By 1858, garment manufacturing was the fastest-growing industry in the city because of the invention of the sewing machine; the need for uniforms during the Civil War, which lasted from 1861 to 1865, created a high demand for jobs as well. The industry continued to thrive through the late 1800s. By 1910, according to Gabriel Montero, the garment industry employed 46 percent of the industrial labor force in New York City. Many garment business owners set up their manufacturing centers in buildings close to the famous retail stores along Fifth Avenue, one of the wealthiest areas of the city.

Fifth Avenue's business owners had a problem: the immigrant workers who walked along the streets and into their shops. The business owners felt that their real estate—which was very valuable—was being compromised and that these lower-class employees were upsetting their wealthy clientele. The famous and influential Fifth Avenue Association finally made a move to push all the immigrant workers out of their area and helped pass zoning laws that would lock the entire garment industry into one segregated section of the city, the area between Ninth Avenue and Broadway, and 34th and 42nd Streets.

she insists. If the Garment Center becomes further diminished, the impact will be felt by the entire fashion industry. According to Guy Trebay, Sui is concerned that "without a production core, it becomes increasingly difficult for young designers to set up shop in the city." Trebay confirms that the situation for the Garment Center looks bleak: "Just a handful of workrooms remain that can whip up custom trimmings, and there are few

That area had a problem of its own: Originally one of the city's most crime-ridden neighborhoods, known for prostitution and drinking, it was nicknamed the Devil's Arcade and the Tenderloin in the late 1800s, long before any fashion entrepreneur had set up shop in its buildings. The Fifth Avenue Association had chosen one of the worst neighborhoods and eyesores in the city for its resolution.

The move, prompted by class discrimination and ethnic discrimination, nonetheless proved to be an important one in the city's history. The hard-working immigrants got busy reforming the neighborhood, establishing unions, and finding work. During World War II, with Paris occupied by Germany, the New York Dress Institute was formed as a collaboration of the mayor, the garment union, and the garment industry to propel New York into being a new center of world fashion. The partnership worked, and the world began to look to the United States for new, innovative fashion designs, such as the development of "sportswear," or separate items that could be easily mixed and matched and that suited the needs of American men and women.

Currently, with many garments being assembled in other countries, like China, jobs in the Garment Center are diminishing and the area has lost much of its former clout. Higher rents, the most recent crisis to hit garment manufacturers, are also pushing many businesses out of the area.

skilled workers capable of operating the bulky machinery required to make gossamer fripperies like Schiffli lace."

"When I was starting, there were wool mills in the U.S. that could make you anything," Sui told Trebay. "The U.S. used to produce the most beautiful cotton denim in the world. Now all that is gone."

To counteract the problem, she joined several other well-known designers, including Vera Wang and Nicole Miller, to heighten the general public's awareness. She launched a campaign in 2008 to "Save the Garment Center," selling black T-shirts that featured that slogan on the front and the e-mail addresses of New York City officials on the back.

In an interview about the importance of the campaign, Sui said:

> I understand that it's all business, but where are we going to go? What are we going to do? In my lifetime, I have seen the area changing, but I can't believe New York can't set aside some building designated to preserving the industry here. . . . The CFDA and many other people have been working to try and come up with a solution for the Garment Center. It's a really difficult process, but the longer it goes on, the more businesses will have to leave because they lost their leases or their landlords are raising rents.

Anna Sui has tackled the problem of the Garment Center with her usual approach—to dive right in and get something done. It was the same approach she took in 1973 as a young woman from the Michigan suburbs, when she was first learning about the fashion industry—she heard about Parsons in New York and decided to move there. It was also the way she launched her first business in 1981 when confronted with the choice of pursuing her endeavor or keeping her job at a junior sportswear company.

As approaches go, hers has proved to be quite successful. There is no reason to think it will not continue to be so.

CHRONOLOGY

1955 Anna Sui is born on August 4 in Detroit, Michigan.

1973 Receives a scholarship to attend the Parsons School of Design.

1975 Leaves Parsons after two years to work in the fashion industry in New York City.

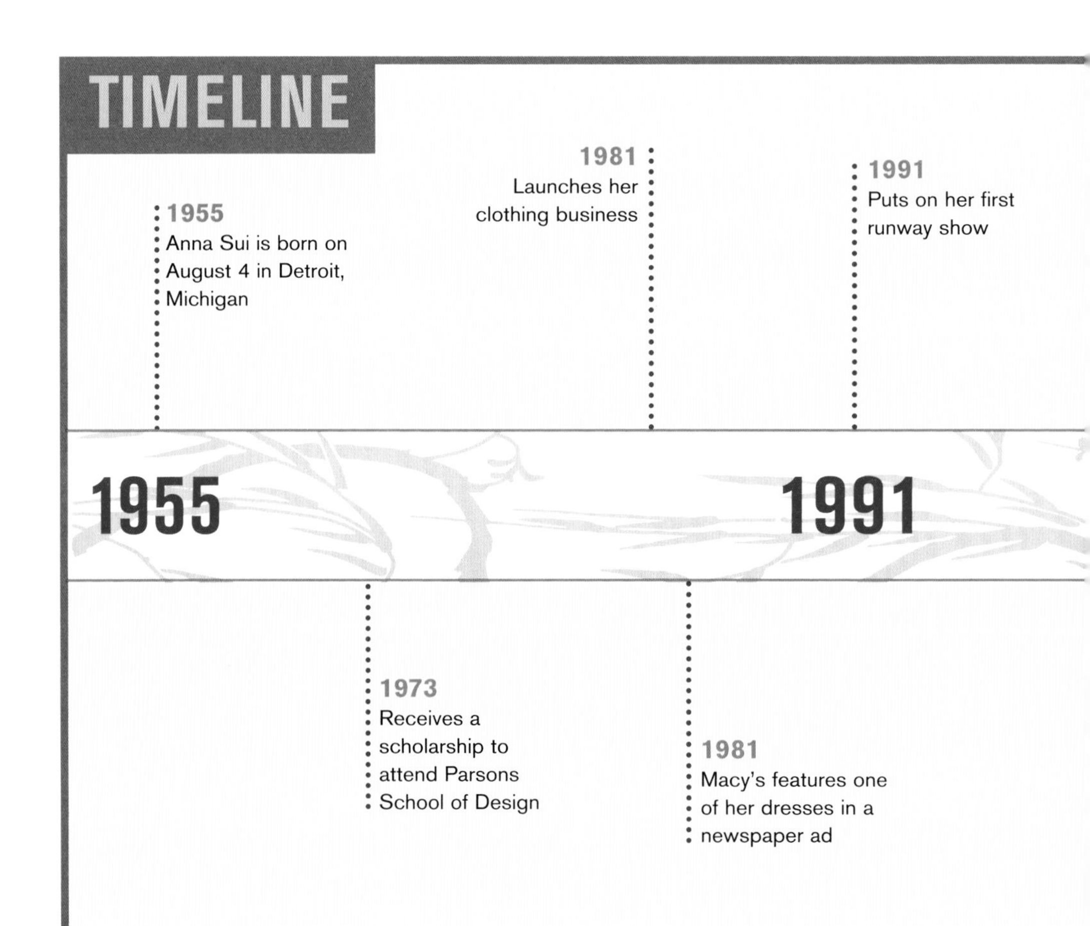

1981 Launches her own clothing business; After Sui attends the Boutique Show, Macy's and Bloomingdale's buy several of her clothes; Macy's features one of her dresses in a newspaper ad.

1988 Moves her line to the Annett B. Showroom.

1991 Madonna and Steven Meisel encourage Sui to put on her first runway show.

1992 Opens her first boutique on Greene Street in SoHo; Macy's gives Sui a 600-square-foot in-store boutique in its flagship Herald Square department store.

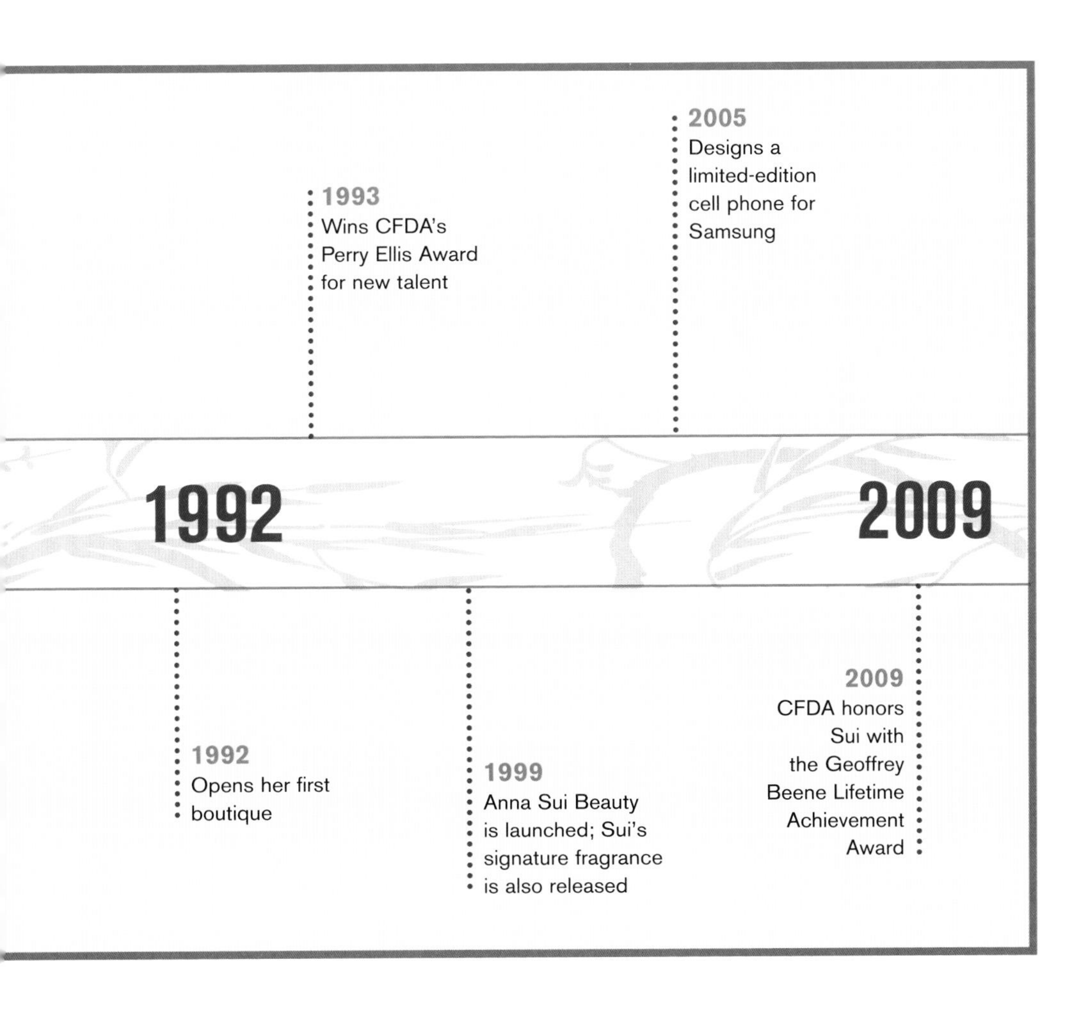

1993 The Council of Fashion Designers of America (CFDA) presents Sui with its Perry Ellis Award for new talent.

1997 Two boutiques open in Japan, where Sui's business is booming; A fragrance and cosmetics deal is signed with the Wella AG and Albion companies; Anna Sui Shoes is launched.

1999 Sui opens another boutique in Los Angeles to cater to her West Coast clientele; Anna Sui Beauty is launched; Sui's signature fragrance is also released.

2000 A new line of skin-care products is launched to accompany Sui's beauty-products line.

2005 Victoria's Secret stores launch Sui's new fragrance, Secret Wish, as an exclusive scent marketed by their company; The flagship boutique on Greene Street in SoHo is doubled in size; Sui's sample collection for her Spring 2006 collection is stolen during a bold theft in New York City; Sui designs a limited-edition cell phone for Samsung.

2006 Creates the Boho Barbie doll for Mattel.

2008 Launches a campaign to "Save the Garment Center" in Manhattan by selling black T-shirts with that slogan on them.

2009 The CFDA honors Sui with the Geoffrey Beene Lifetime Achievement Award.

GLOSSARY

androgynous—The mixing of masculine and feminine traits; the look was popular in the 1960s and 1970s as a form of social rebellion.

Bohemian—Originally, Bohemian referred to the people of Bohemia, but the term came to be applied to the Gypsies, or Roma people, who traveled through Bohemia; later, the term was used (as a derogatory one) to describe European artists, musicians, writers, and other creative people who lived an untraditional lifestyle. Today, the term describes a fashion look that is unorthodox, eccentric, and original, such as the "hippie" look of the 1960s.

chinoiserie—A style in art (as in decoration) that reflects Chinese qualities or motifs.

couture—From the French word for "sewing," couture refers to both the business of designing clothing and to the clothes themselves. Likewise, "haute couture" (from the French for "high sewing") refers to the more famous and exclusive fashion houses, designers, and clothes.

dolly bird—The look of the modern, urban girl in 1960s "swinging" London, typified by a thin build, miniskirt, and short, androgynous hair.

fashion collection—The series of clothing items produced by a fashion designer or a design company, intended for display and sale during either the fall or spring season each year. Collections usually have a theme or specific influence that gives the items a unified look.

fashion design—An applied art that seeks to create clothing and accessories that reflect the social, cultural, and even political influences of a specific time period.

Fashion Week—An important series of fashion events (shows, displays, media events) that takes place twice a year, in the fall and the spring, in New York City

Garment Center—Historic district in Manhattan (between Broadway and Ninth Avenue, and between 34th and 42nd Streets) that has been the center of manufacturing clothing since 1919.

goth—A style of dress, music, and literature that is inspired by Victorian, romantic, and morbid influences; the look is typified by the color black and often dramatic makeup and hairstyles.

Greenwich Village—The neighborhood in Manhattan below 14th Street and west of Broadway; a mostly residential area, it has an artistic reputation and an active cultural scene.

kitsch—Art that is considered inferior, lowbrow, or aesthetically unpleasing.

punk rock—An offshoot of rock 'n' roll that developed in the 1970s; punk musicians saw rock musicians as becoming too mainstream and excessive, and so they sought to produce edgy music often with anti-authoritarian messages.

ready to wear—A fashion-industry term that refers to clothing that does not need to be tailored to individual body types or sizes. It is "ready to wear" off the hanger and sold by sizes. Also known as prêt-a-porter.

rock 'n' roll—A popular musical style, based on jazz, blues, folk music, and other genres, that emerged in the 1950s and developed in the 1960s; rock 'n' roll relied on electronic instruments, especially the electric guitar, for its signature sound.

runway show—A fashion show in which models display clothing while walking on an elevated platform, known as a runway or a catwalk.

SoHo—An abbreviation of "South of Houston Street," or the neighborhood below Houston Street in Manhattan that is known for its shops, studios, and cultural and artistic life.

sportswear—Also known as "active wear" or "separates," sportswear was created by American designers as a way to cater to the needs of active, young, working people. The basic concept is to have several separate pieces—blouses, pants, skirts, jackets, and accessories—that can be mixed and matched for easy-to-assemble looks. The casual look is meant to be comfortable but still stylish.

BIBLIOGRAPHY

Allis, Tim. "The Sui Smell of Success." *People*. July 13, 1992. Available online. URL: http://www.people.com/people/archive/article/0,,20113090,00.htm.

"Anna Sui Biography." Anna Sui's Official Web site. Available online. URL: http://www.AnnaSui.com.

"Anna Sui: Serious Business Has Its Sunny Side." *Global Cosmetic Industry*. July 2004. Vol 172 (7).

"Asia Society Presents 'Burn It Up': Breakout Asian-American Designers in Fashion." Asia Society. Available online. URL: http://www.asiasociety.org/pressroom/rel-burnitup.html.

Ballentine, Sandra. "Timeless: Jet Set." *The New York Times*. September 24, 2006. Available online. URL: http://www.nytimes.com/2006/09/24/travel/tmagazine/24timeless.html.

Blain, Joanne. "Cult Classic: Quirky Designer Anna Sui Will Make Her First Trip to Vancouver This Week." *The Vancouver Sun*. November 6, 2007.

———. "The Quirky Mind of Anna Sui: Michigan-Born Designer Says Fashion About Spirit." *The Windsor Star*. November 17, 2007.

Bumpus, Jessica. "Sui Dreams." *Vogue*. August 21, 2008. Available online. URL: http://www.vogue.co.uk/news/daily/080821-anna-suis-garment-centre-tshirt.aspx.

Craik, Laura. "Sixties Summertime as Sui Does Happy Hippy Shapes." *Evening Standard*. September 11, 2008.

DeCarlo, Lauren. "Annett B. Calls It a Day." *WWD*. July 21, 2005.

Fortini, Amanda. "How the Runway Took Off: A Brief History of the Fashion Show." *Slate*. February 8, 2006. Available online. URL: http://www.slate.com/id/2135561.

Goddard, Joanna. "Heaven, with Hangers." *New York*. August 17, 2008. Available online. URL: http://nymag.com/fashion/08/fall/49258/.

Gordon, Mary Ellen. "Anna Sui." Fashion Encyclopedia. Available online. URL: http://www.fashionencyclopedia.com/Sp-To/Sui-Anna.html.

Grawe, Sam. "Alexander the Great." *Dwell*. February 2008.

Hahn, Lorraine. "Fashion Designer Anna Sui's Talk Asia Interview Transcript." CNN.com. August 6, 2004. Available online. URL: http://www.cnn.com/2004/WORLD/asiapcf/08/06/talkasia.sui.script/index.html.

"Haute Couture." *Time*. August 13, 1934. Available online. URL: http://www.time.com/time/printout/0,8816,747679,00.html.

Hirano, Koji. "Anna Sui Aiming Young in Japan." *WWD*. May 22, 2007. Vol. 193(110).

Horyn, Cathy. "Adventures in a Girl's Life with Anna Sui." *The New York Times*. September 15, 2006. Available online. URL: http://www.nytimes.com/2006/09/15/fashion/shows/15FASH.html?fta=y.

Karimzadeh, Marc. "Anna Sui Opens Up With Larger Store." *WWD*. November 14, 2005. Vol. 190 (105).

———. "Anna Sui Sample Collection Stolen in NYC." *WWD*. September 21, 2005. Vol. 190(63).

Kuczynski, Alex. "Journey Back to a Wild and Crazy Time." *The New York Times*. March 30, 2006. Available online. URL: http://www.nytimes.com/2006/03/30/fashion/thursdaystyles/30CRITIC.html.

Lackie, Dave. "Anna Sui: Alt Icon, Goth Culture's Fave Designer." *National Post*. November 11, 2006.

Menkes, Suzy. "Women Pioneered East Meets West." *International Herald Tribune*. September 9, 2008.

Montero, Gabriel. "A Stitch in Time: A History of New York's Fashion District." Fashion Center Business Improvement District, 2008. Available online. URL: http://www.fashioncenter.com/history/index.html.

Morra, Bernadette. "Anna Sui, the Ageless Wild Child." *Toronto Star*. November 2, 2006. Available online. URL: http://www.thestar.com/article/114375.

"Nail Colour from Anna Sui Beauty." *Cosmetics*. Don Mills: January/February 2005. Vol. 33(1).

Naughton, Julie, and Brid Costello. "Anna Sui's Got a Secret." *WWD*. April 1, 2008.

Nevitt, Naomi. "Alexander Wang." *Teen Vogue*. Available online. URL: http://www.teenvogue.com/industry/designer/AlexanderWang.

"New York Fashion Week: Anna Sui Spring 2009 Fashion Show." Groove Effect Web site. Available online. URL: http://www.grooveeffect.com/w-style/091408-new-york-fashion-week-anna-s.php.

Norwich, William. "Sui Generous: Caviar, Cocktails, and Clothes Make for Fine Conversation at Anna Sui's." *New York Times Magazine*. Fall 2000. Available online. URL: http://partners.nytimes.com/library/magazine/specials/20001029mag-norwich22.html.

Owens, Mitchell. "David Hicks, 69, Interior Design Star of the 60s, Is Dead." *The New York Times*. April 2, 1998. Available online. URL: http://query.nytimes.com/gst/fullpage.html?res=9900E0DC163AF931A35757C0A96E958260.

Ozzard, Janet. "Anna Sui, Fall 2004 Ready-to-Wear: Review." Style.com. February 11, 2004. Available online. URL: http://www.style.com/fashionshows/review/F2004RTW ANNASUI/.

Parker, Eloise. "Hippest and Hautest; New York Designer Anna Sui Is Always in Fashion." New York *Daily News*. September 5, 2007.

Parsons The New School for Design Web site. Available online. URL: http://www.parsons.edu.

Phelps, Nicole. "Anna Sui, Fall 2005 Ready-to-Wear: Review." Style.com. February 9, 2005. Available online. URL: http://www.style.com/fashionshows/review/F2005RTW-ANNASUI.

———. "Anna Sui, Spring 2009 Ready-to-Wear: Review." Style.com. September 10, 2008. Available online. URL: http://www.style.com/fashionshows/review/S2009RTW-ANNASUI.

"Samsung Launches Anna Sui Couture Phone." *Wireless News*. February 21, 2005.

Schiro, Anne-Marie. "Anna Sui Pounds Out the Beat." *The New York Times*. November 5, 1993. Available online. URL: http://www.nytimes.com/1993/11/05/news/reviews-fashion-anna-sui-pounds-out-the-beat.html.

Seidler, Benj Ohad. "Fashion Never Smelt So Sui." *Varsity*. November 18, 2005. Available online. URL: http://www.varsity.co.uk/archive/628.pdf.

Seymour, Kristen. "Anna Sui Wants to Save the Garment Center, with a Tee." *StyleList*. August 23, 2008. Available online. URL:

http://www.stylelist.com/blog/2008/08/23/anna-sui-wants-to-save-the-garment-center-with-a-tee/.

"Shocking! The Art and Fashion of Elsa Schiaparelli." Philadelphia Museum of Art. Available online. URL: http://www.philamuseum.org/micro_sites/exhibitions/schiaparelli/tour/index.htm.

Sui, Anna. "From New York to Tokyo, She Knows What Women Want." *Newsweek*. October 13, 2008. Vol 152 (15).

———. "It's Only Rock & Roll . . ." *InStyle*. October 2002. Vol 9(11).

"Sui Dreams." *Cosmo Girl*. May 1, 2007.

"Sui Generis." AsiaMs.net. Available online. URL: http://asiams.net/Fashion/SuiAnna/sui.html.

Trebay, Guy. "Testing Her Strong Suit." *The New York Times*. February 11, 2009. Available online. URL: http://www.nytimes.com/2009/02/12/fashion/12runway.html?partner=rss.

White, Rosie. *Violent Femmes: Women as Spies in Popular Culture*. London: Routledge, 2007.

FURTHER RESOURCES

BOOKS

Burke, Sandra. *Fashion Artist: Drawing Techniques to Portfolio Presentation* (Fashion Design Series). Burke Publishing, 2006.

Gap Min, Pyong. *Asian Americans: Contemporary Trends and Issues*. Thousand Oaks, Calif.: Pine Forge Press, 2006.

Gehlhar, Mary. *The Fashion Designer Survival Guide: Start and Run Your Own Fashion Business*. New York: Kaplan Publishing, 2008.

Tatham, Caroline, and Julian Seaman. *Fashion Design Drawing Course*. Hauppauge, N.Y.: Barron's Educational Series, 2003.

Zia, Helen. *Asian American Dreams: The Emergence of an American People*. New York: Farrar, Straus and Giroux, 2001.

WEB SITES

Anna Sui
http://www.annasui.com

Asian Nation: Asian American History, Demographics, and Issues.
http://www.AsianNation.org

Fashion Encyclopedia
http://www.fashionencyclopedia.com

PHOTO CREDITS

page:

11: John Angelillo/UPI/ Landov
15: AP Images/Jennifer Graylock
21: AP Images
26: AP Images/Jennifer Graylock
31: AP Images/Jim Cooper
40: Mike Segar/Reuters/Landov
48: Time & Life Pictures/ Getty Images
55: Getty Images
60: AP Images/Mary Altaffer
63: AP Images
70: AP Images/Seth Wenig
76: AP Images/Kathy Willens
79: AP Images/Jennifer Graylock
81: Keith Bedford/Reuters/ Landov
85: AP Images/Jennifer Graylock
89: AFP/Getty Images
94: AP Images/Stephen Chernin
96: Getty Images
99: AP Images/Jennifer Graylock

INDEX

ABOUT THE AUTHOR

SUSAN MUADDI DARRAJ is associate professor of English at Harford Community College in Bel Air, Maryland, and senior editor of *The Baltimore Review*, a literary journal of fiction, poetry, and essays. She has authored several biographies for Chelsea House Publishers. Her short-fiction collection, *The Inheritance of Exile*, was published in 2007. She lives in Baltimore, Maryland, with her husband and three children.